WILL THIS BE
CANADA'S CENTURY?

To Joyce
With many thanks for
supporting Friends
Paul Schafer

WILL THIS BE
CANADA'S CENTURY?

D. Paul Schafer

Rock's Mills Press

Oakville, Ontario

PUBLISHED BY

Rock's Mills Press

Copyright © 2017 by D. Paul Schafer
PUBLISHED BY ARRANGEMENT WITH THE AUTHOR • ALL RIGHTS RESERVED

Library and Archives Canada Cataloguing in Publication is available from the publisher.
Email Rock's Mills Press at customer.service@rocksmillspress.com.

Contents

Preface

Will this be Canada's century? Many Canadians have asked themselves this question ever since Wilfrid Laurier predicted that the twentieth century would belong to Canada—or words to that effect—in a speech he gave to the Canadian Club in Ottawa in 1904.

While Laurier was wrong about his prediction—the twentieth century obviously belonged to the United States and in every conceivable way—is there any possibility that the twenty-first century could be Canada's century?

Most people would probably say "decidedly not." In the sense in which we have come to understand what it means for a century to "belong" to a country—that is to say, for a country to achieve a high standard of living, possess a great deal of economic, military, commercial, and financial power, and play the dominant role in the world—most people and likely most Canadians would say that the twenty-first century will belong to China or India. These countries have huge populations, enormous consumer markets, and are growing at rapid rates in economic terms (even if these rates have slowed somewhat in recent years). Indeed, the world's centre of gravity seems to be shifting from west to east. While the future is always an open book, China and India are probably the "best bets" for having the twenty-first century belong to them.

And yet, this type of thinking is based on the current way of looking at things and on the way things have been done in the past. The problem is that looking at matters in this way is no longer sustainable, either for individual countries or for the world as a whole. This has become painfully apparent as a result of climate change, the environmental crisis, huge disparities in income and wealth, the migration of millions of people, numerous immigration and refugee problems, terrorism and terrorist attacks, and conflicts between different peoples, groups, countries, religions, and civilizations. It doesn't take a psychic to depict the kind of world that could result in the not-too-distant future as world population increases, natural resources are used up, unsustainable demands are made on the natural environment, and the finite carrying capacity of the earth is approached. Due to these and other problems, it is evident that things must change— *and change substantially*—if human survival and environmental well-being are to be assured in the future. Maintaining the status quo and staying the course are no longer options. The costs, consequences, and dangers are too great.

Clearly a new course must be charted for humanity and brought into being if these problems are to be addressed successfully in the future. This course must be capable of creating a very different type of relationship between human beings and the natural environment, reducing the enormous disparities that exist in income and wealth, decreasing poverty, increasing employment, coming to grips with climate change and social, economic, and political injustices, improving relations between the diverse peoples, countries, races, religions, and cultures of the world, and creating a great deal more happiness, peace, harmony, and security in life.

Can Canada play a leadership role in charting this new course for humanity and making it a reality? If so, it might just be possible for the twenty-first century to belong to Canada, despite the fact that the country lacks a vast population or gigantic market.

In order for Canada to play such a role, a chronological and cultural approach to Canadian development is required, rather than a contemporary and partial approach. The value of the chronological approach is threefold: it allows us to see clearly how Canada has evolved in the past and what is most essential to learn from this; it shows where Canada and the world stand at present and what are the most pressing problems facing the country and the world today; and it helps determine where Canada should be headed in the future. The cultural approach is needed to focus attention on the big picture and not just specific parts of it, as well as to ascertain how Canadian culture can be developed most effectively in the years and decades ahead.

When considered in this chronological and cultural manner, it is clear that Canada is capable of playing a leadership role in the world of the future, largely by making the changes in worldviews, values, lifestyles, and individual and collective behaviour that are imperative for this. However, Canada would not be acting as an empire-builder in the traditional sense, but, rather, as an exemplar in the forward-looking and future-oriented sense.

Such a course of action is vital for many reasons: to achieve sustainable development; to come to grips with climate change and the environmental crisis; to reduce the major inequalities that exist in income and wealth; to create acceptable standards of living and a decent quality of life; to enable the country and its citizenry to play a proactive and seminal rather than reactive and imitative role in the world; and to make Canada and the world better and safer places in which to live, work, develop, interact, and thrive.

In order to do this, it will be necessary to capitalize on some of Canada's greatest historical and contemporary assets, most notably the ability to create and maintain a strong and independent country against virtually insurmountable odds, manifest a great deal of creativity, deal with an incredible amount of diversity, and create a distinct way of life. It will also be necessary to strike out in some bold, new, and daring directions in the future—directions that are finely tuned to the needs and aspirations of Canada, Canadians, people and countries in other parts of the world, and the world as a whole.

It is impossible to write a book of this type without receiving help and support from many people. First of all, I would like to thank my family—my wife Nancy and daughters Charlene and Susan—for their companionship and encouragement during the research and writing of this book. I would also like to thank my children's godparents, Attila and Elfriede, and my brother Murray and his wife Eleanor, as well as many close friends and colleagues, including André Fortier, John Hobday, Sheila Jans, Joyce Zemans, Frank Pasquill, Peter Sever, Leslie Oliver, Barry Witkin, John Gordon, Real Bedard, Stephen Thorne, Joy MacFadyen, Don McGregor, Biserka Cvjetičanin, Galyna Shevchenko, Gao Xian, Diane Dodd, Herman Greene, Ashfaq Ishaq, Grant Hall, and many others, for their on-going commitment to my work on culture in general and Canadian culture in particular.

I would especially like to thank Walter Pitman for the indispensable role he played in the evolution of the book. We worked on a rough draft of the book on a part-time basis shortly after the twenty-first century began. Unfortunately, we were unable to continue our work on the book as a result of other commitments and responsibilities we had at that time. When I was able to return to the book and work on it on a full-time basis, more than ten years had elapsed and a great deal had changed in Canada and the world. Moreover, Walter was no longer able to work on the book due to some very difficult health problems. However, he encouraged me to continue with the book on my own and make all the necessary changes that were required to update the manuscript, rewrite or revise all the chapters, clarify and strengthen the arguments, and add much new material. While accepting responsibility for all these changes and the overall character and contents of the book, I am most grateful to Walter for his valuable contributions to the book, as well as urging me to do what was necessary to complete the book and get it published. Without his help, encouragement, and support, this book would not exist.

The fact that it does exist owes a great deal to David Stover. Not only did David express a keen interest in the book and a strong commitment to it, but also he edited the book, designed the covers, and published it through his publishing house, Rock's Mills Press. I have worked with David on a number of other books I have written on culture and Canadian creativity and can say without reservation or qualification that this has been one of the most enjoyable, productive, and rewarding experiences in my life. I am very grateful for this.

D. Paul Schafer
Markham, Ontario
2017

A nation's culture resides
in the hearts and in the soul of its people.

MAHATMA GANDHI

CHAPTER ONE

Right Idea, Wrong Century

*Canada has been modest in its history, although its history, in my
estimation, is only commencing. It is commencing in this century. The
nineteenth century was the century of the United States. I think we can
claim that Canada will fill the twentieth century.*

—Sir Wilfrid Laurier, January 18, 1904

In 1904, Sir Wilfrid Laurier made a famous speech to the Canadian
Club in Ottawa. In it, he claimed that "Canada will fill the twentieth
century." It was a bold and imaginative idea, one that was
interpreted by many Canadians to mean that the twentieth century would
belong to Canada.

This idea was far more than political rhetoric left over from a highly
successful election campaign that had returned Laurier as prime minister
and his government to power. Laurier actually believed that the country
was standing on the threshold of a whole new era, one that would see
remarkable changes in Canada, Canadians, and Canada's role in the world.

Laurier's optimism was not unfounded. He had seen Canada grow
rapidly in the latter decades of the nineteenth century and first few years
of the new century. The country's population was expanding quickly, the
west was filling up with immigrants from abroad, the Canadian Pacific
Railway had just been built, and numerous towns and cities were booming
across the country, from Halifax and Saint John in the east to Montreal,
Quebec City, Toronto, and Winnipeg in the centre and Calgary, Edmonton, and Vancouver in the west. There were also strong signs of industrial
and agricultural growth, spurred on by high tariffs and the National Policy
introduced by Sir John A. Macdonald several decades earlier.

There is no doubt that Laurier's understanding of what it meant to "fill
a century" was industrial, military, and political in character, since it was

intimately tied up with notions of economic growth, military might, and "empires" that Laurier also talked about in his speech. He contended that the nineteenth century was the century of the United States. In a speech he gave at Toronto's Massey Hall in October 1904, he said: "I tell you nothing but what you know when I tell you that the nineteenth century has been the century of United States development. The past hundred years has been filled with the pages of their history. Let me tell you, my fellow countrymen, that the twentieth century shall be the century of Canada and of Canadian development. For the next seventy-five years, nay for the next hundred years, Canada shall be the star towards which all men who love progress and freedom shall come."

It would seem that history and hindsight have proven Laurier wrong. Even his assertion that the nineteenth century belonged to the United States would be challenged by many scholars. Indeed, it was during the nineteenth century that Britain reached the height of its power. After the defeat of Napoleon, Britannia "ruled the waves," extending its empire over so many countries and parts of the world beyond the "tight little island" that maps of the world had to be perpetually redrawn with more and more swatches of pink. It was said that the sun never set on the British Empire. When, in 1858, Britain took over direct rule of India from the East India Company, fully one-quarter of the world's population lived under British rule. Even today, this vast empire remains a source of inspiration during such events as the "Last Night of the Proms" concerts at the Royal Albert Hall in London, where thousands of normally restrained concert goers don red, white, and blue hats and Union Jack T-shirts and sing *Rule Britannia*, Elgar's *Land of Hope and Glory*, and Parry's *Jerusalem* with great gusto but also a touch of nostalgia for an era and an empire long gone.

Nevertheless, Laurier may have seen something in 1904 that the vast expanse of the British Empire obscured for many. During the nineteenth century, the United States was largely preoccupied with its own internal affairs—westward expansion, rapid population and economic growth, and, of course, the Civil War. It played relatively little part in the geopolitical machinations of the European empires. By 1890, however, the United States had surpassed Britain as the world's largest manufacturer, and by the end of the nineteenth century the American economy was the largest in the world. In 1900, American gross national product on a per capita basis was 50 percent higher than in Britain and double that of most Western European countries. If the nineteenth century belonged to Britain, the foundations were laid that would vault the United States to dominance in the twentieth century and make that century, in the words of the American publisher Henry Luce, the "American century."

What, then, of Laurier's belief that Canada would "fill the twentieth century"?

Although Laurier was an astute and perceptive politician, no more than any other man did he possess the power of prophecy. Tumultuous events shaped and dominated the twentieth century, including two world wars, the global economic depression of the 1930s, the Cold War between the United States and the USSR that divided the world between capitalism and communism, and, at the very end of the century, globalization, computerization, and the creation of huge free trade zones.

Laurier was also unable to predict the limitations that would be imposed on Canada by virtue of its small population, modest industrial and manufacturing base and markets, heavy reliance on natural resources and the extraction industries, and dependence on foreign capital. A small population seeking to develop a colossal land mass in a relatively inhospitable environment posed enough problems; playing a major role in two world wars and losing a significant number of citizens and potential leaders in the process imposed even greater burdens.

However, an incredible amount *was* achieved by Canada in the twentieth century. As noted, Canada played a vital role in both world wars, particularly World War II. Between the wars, a major depression was confronted and overcome, as was a terrible drought on the prairies that devastated western farms and farmers. The country's population grew from roughly five million at the beginning of the century to thirty million by the end, and countless immigrants and refugees were absorbed into Canadian society without a great deal of friction or difficulty. Moreover, the country's standard of living and quality of life rose dramatically, the educational system was enlarged and revitalized, a social system was created that included public health care, pensions, old-age security, worker's compensation, welfare payments, and major advances in the individual and collective rights and freedoms of Canadians.

And this was not all. An artistic renaissance occurred in the latter part of the twentieth century that was spurred on by the Massey Commission from 1949 to 1951, the creation of the Canada Council in 1957, and Expo and the centennial celebrations in 1967. Canadian artists and arts organizations achieved remarkable results at home and abroad. The country was also successful in making the transition from a traditional agricultural and rural society to a modern industrial and urban society. Despite the country's small population, Canada's economy was the eighth largest in the world in the year 2000, and Canada was selected "the best country in the world in which to live" by the United Nations. Based on these accomplishments, Laurier could undoubtedly have justified his prediction.

Nonetheless, much was *not* accomplished in the twentieth century. The country's Indigenous peoples were forced to endure countless hardships and difficulties, tensions and conflicts existed between French and English Canadians, major inequalities in income and wealth persisted and even worsened, especially towards the end of the century, the environmental situation deteriorated, and more homeless people appeared on city streets. Internationally, at the end of the century Canada did not play the role in the world many Canadians thought it would and should.

As the twentieth century ended and the twenty-first century began, two books appeared that were germane to Laurier's prediction. The first was *Our Country* by J.L. Granatstein and Robert Bothwell, two distinguished and well-known Canadian historians. They claimed that Canada had done very well in the twentieth century and was well positioned for the twenty-first. The authors concluded that Canada had been "a success in a minor key" and "we can and should believe that we had the best of it."

The other book, *Our Vanishing Country*, was written by Mel Hurtig, publisher of the Canadian Encyclopedia and one of the principal founders of the Council of Canadians and several other important organizations. His book was far less hopeful. While admitting that a great deal had been achieved in the early and middle decades of the twentieth century, Hurtig went on to say that the "selling-off" and "selling-out" of Canada by the country's corporate and political elites—as well as the "hollowing out of the Canadian economy" due to the signing of the Canada-U.S. and then North American free trade agreements—threatened the future existence of the country. His book was a stinging indictment. It was also a reminder (as if one were needed) that the twentieth century had clearly belonged to the United States. Over the course of the century, the United States shaped and led the world in virtually all sectors of public and private life, creating an extremely high standard of living and quality of life for its people. Indeed, the U.S. became by far the most powerful nation on earth and, according to some historians, the most powerful nation that had ever existed. No other country matched its prowess. It was in a class by itself, without equal.

Despite their divergent views, Granatstein, Bothwell, and Hurtig confirmed that a great deal was accomplished in the twentieth century that would stand Canada and Canadians in good stead in the twenty-first century. The country's diverse population, creative accomplishments, dynamic economy, healthy labour force, and highly developed social, educational, and governmental institutions, systems, and programs were all strengths that could be capitalized on in the years and decades ahead. However, Canada suffered from some serious shortcomings that would have to be dealt with in the future. Among these were rapidly escalating environmental problems, overdependence on foreign capital and natural resource extraction, and an apparent inability (or unwillingness) to play a strong role in the world.

The twenty-first century is shaping up to be even more difficult and demanding than the twentieth. While the beginning of the twentieth century gave rise to a great deal of optimism and enthusiasm—the First World War was still a decade in the future when Laurier gave his famous speech—the start of the present century produced a great deal of anxiety and apprehension among Canadians as well as among people elsewhere in the world. This pessimism is due to a number of factors.

Domestically, Canada is a much more diversified and complicated country today than it was in Laurier's day. Many institutions and systems were created over the last century and especially since the Second World War that did not exist in 1900. These institutions and systems—in economics, health care, education, the environment, social welfare, recreation, communications, the arts, sciences, technology, security, and so on—will have to be judiciously managed if they are to serve Canada and Canadians to best advantage in the future. Moreover, the country and its citizenry are confronted with difficult new challenges that did not exist at the beginning of the twentieth century—pollution, urban sprawl, transportation gridlock, increasing inequalities, slow economic growth, and an aging population.

But it is the world situation that is causing even more anxiety and apprehension. A matrix of problems has emerged that seems beyond the control of established international structures, systems, and institutions. Global warming, huge disparities in income and wealth, terrorism, escalating tensions between countries, ethnic groups, and religions, the spread of infectious diseases, and the threat of nuclear, chemical, and biological warfare all hang ominously over humanity.

Clearly the world has become much more volatile and unstable over the last few decades. Much of this instability has to do with the fact that the population of the world is growing rapidly and there are many more interactions occurring among its diverse peoples, countries, cultures, and religions. Globalization, free trade, the invasions of Iraq and Afghanistan, conflicts in the Middle East and in Africa, Asia, and Latin America, and the rise of right-wing populist movements (including the election of Donald Trump in the United States) are revealing that profound differences exist in the way people see, interpret, understand, and act in the world. This is the new global reality, and it would be foolish to underestimate or ignore it.

Canada and Canadians are no strangers to this new reality. By virtue of their historical development and contemporary character, the country and its citizenry have had a great deal of experience with the problems and possibilities, both painful and pleasant, that result from interactions between people with very different origins, experiences, values, beliefs, and ways of life. Relations between the Indigenous peoples and other Canadians, the long and protracted difficulties between French and English Canadians, and experiences with immigrants from all parts of the globe have produced a country and a people strongly committed to multiculturalism and pluralism, respect for cultural differences, the rights of citizens, and the need for integration and cooperation rather than assimilation, conflict, and confrontation. All of this has given Canadians valuable insights into how peaceful relations can be achieved between people from vastly different cultures, as well as the role that Canada can play as a microcosm of the global macrocosm.

Such insights will be needed in the twenty-first century. For standing behind the aforementioned problems is one much more fundamental, debilitating, and potentially life-threatening. With the globe's population at seven billion and still growing, and with consumerism and the marketplace making incredible demands on the environment, the entire global system could become much more unstable and even collapse if ways are not found to counteract or prevent it.

A new course will have to be charted for humanity if this potentially explosive situation is to be dealt with successfully. This will require ideas, values, behaviours, and actions very different from those that dominate Canada and the world today. The existing world system will not solve these problems. Humanity must come to grips with the ecological crisis, terrorism, racism, and the perpetual threat of a nuclear, chemical, or biological catastrophe. It will also have to produce economies that are clean, green, creative, sustainable, and shared, eliminate huge disparities in income and wealth, promote safety, security, and peace, cultivate new sources of energy, open up opportunities for young people to participate actively in all future planetary developments, improve the status of women and girls, deal effectively with immigration and the refugee crisis, and make it possible for *all* people and *all* countries to enjoy reasonable standards of living and a decent quality of life with straining the globe's scarce resources and finite carrying capacity to the breaking point.

Can Canada play a seminal role in charting this new course for humanity? Most people would probably say "no" because the population of the country is too small. However, dig a little deeper and it becomes apparent that the country and its citizenry possess many of the qualities, capabilities, and characteristics necessary to make this new course for humanity a reality.

In historical terms, Canadians have created a strong, independent, and sovereign country despite insurmountable odds, exhibited an incredible amount of creativity, manifested a great deal of caring, sharing, compassion, and kindness, dealt with complexity and diversity, and evolved a distinct culture, economy, and way of life. They have also demonstrated a remarkable capacity for getting along well with others and working cooperatively with other people and other countries, despite major differences in languages, beliefs, values, ethnic origins, social customs, and cultural traditions.

It is not only in the historical sense that Canada and Canadians possess many of the requirements that are necessary to chart this new course for humanity. Despite the many challenges facing the country, there is room for optimism with respect to the future. This optimism stems from the creative achievements and myriad accomplishments that Canada and Canadians have realized over the centuries in transportation, communications, resource development, the arts, sciences, technology, education, sports, politics, recreation, and many other fields.

Clearly there is a quiet sense of confidence building in Canada and among Canadians. Spurred on by the election of the Liberal government in 2015, the artistic transformation that is taking place in all parts of the country, the numerous accolades that have been conferred on Canadian artists, arts organizations, and academics at home and abroad, the many accomplishments by the country's athletes at the Olympic Games, the Pan Am Games, and numerous world championships, and the feeling that the country does not have to take a back seat to Britain, France, the United States, or any other country, this rapidly evolving sense of confidence is based on the belief that it is time for Canada and Canadians to step forward and make their mark on the world.

By creating a dynamic, decent, humane, and progressive country and culture at home and contributing significantly to the welfare and well-being of millions of people and numerous countries in other parts of the world, a major step will be taken towards the realization of a better Canada and a better world. Balance, harmony, sustainability, equality, tolerance, and inclusion—rather than conflict, excess, oppression, inequality, and exclusion—are the touchstones of this better Canada and better world.

The best way for Canadians to achieve this goal and fulfill their potential is to play an exemplary role in the world. This is what George Woodcock, one of Canada's most respected scholars, contended many years ago, when he said that the country and its citizenry possess the potential to play a seminal role in the world as an "exemplar." This means setting a good example for other people and countries to follow, as well as achieving a lot with a little and producing concrete results with the least amount of friction, fall-out, and conflict. This has always been a fundamental feature of Canadian culture, as well as one of the country's most important assets.

The world is watching to see if Canada can deal effectively with its domestic and international problems, possibilities, and responsibilities. If the country and its citizens can stand up and be counted on matters of conscience and character, maintain their objectivity and independence while living next door to the United States, the most powerful nation on earth, live in harmony with the natural environment and each other, create a more just, equitable, and inclusive society, increase foreign aid and developmental assistance substantially, participate actively in the settlement of immigrants and refugees, and make beneficial contributions to improving the state of the natural environment and the well-being of people and countries elsewhere in the world, then the twenty-first century could very well "belong to Canada."

Some of Canada's finest hours have come when, in spite of good relations with its mother countries, France and Britain, as well as its next-door neighbour the United States, Canadians have stood up for values, principles, and ideals that transcend these relationships. There are many examples. One was Lester Pearson playing a crucial role in finding a solution to the 1956 Suez Crisis, after the United Kingdom and France took the drastic step of military action in the wake of the take-over of this strategic facility by Egypt. Another was foreign affairs minister Lloyd Axworthy providing the impetus and a venue for the adoption of the 1996 Ottawa

Treaty, which led to an international ban on anti-personnel land mines. And yet another was when the federal government decided not to join the United States in the invasion of Iraq because proof was not provided that Iraq was harbouring weapons of mass destruction.

It is examples like these, particularly when combined with the many other strengths, assets, and capabilities that Canada and Canadians possess, that prove that the country is capable of punching "far above its weight" and can be a real "game changer" in the twenty-first century. For what the world needs is not "more of the same," but rather a fundamental change in direction, especially with respect to the creation of ideas, ideals, lifestyles, and modes of behaviour that are consistent with Canadian and global requirements and realities in the years and decades ahead.

While Canada will be challenged in the twenty-first century by some heavy hitters with huge populations and colossal markets, including China, India, and Brazil, as well as by the presence of the United States on its doorstep, Canada need not have a huge population or market to have a "century belong to it," as indeed Great Britain—by no means the largest country in the world or even in Europe—proved in the nineteenth century. All Canada and Canadians need to do to play an exemplary role in the world is to change existing ways of doing things in such a way that they are compatible with the needs of the twenty-first century, particularly with respect to the relationship with the natural environment as well as relations among diverse peoples, religions, and cultures.

Such a development would help create a world where peace, harmony, equality, and well-being are not just empty words or wishful thinking, but, rather, the foundations of a new Canadian and global reality. To do so would not only realize Laurier's dream, but would do so in a way that is consistent with the country's past development, present circumstances, and future needs. For as John McHale, the distinguished futurist, artist, and visionary once said, "people survive, uniquely, by their capacity to act in the present on the basis of past experiences considered in terms of future consequences."

CHAPTER TWO

A Country Despite Incredible Odds

T he creation of Canada as a strong and sovereign country in the northern half of the North America continent has often been described as a miracle. That a small and scattered population has been able to create and maintain a country stretching across five and a half of the globe's twenty-four time zones—a country second in the world in geographical area only to Russia—must be considered a remarkable achievement.

Both the Indigenous peoples and first European settlers were forced to confront and overcome the colossal size and inhospitable nature of what would become Canada. As the country grew, other challenges included the need to establish an east-west transportation and communications axis contrary to the north-south pull of North American geography, countless struggles between French and English colonists, and the constant threat from south of the border as the American colonies joined together to form the United States and pushed relentlessly northward and westward.

Even after the Dominion of Canada was formed by the British North America Act in 1867, endless problems remained to be overcome—problems that threatened the country's newfound independence. Among them were complaints by the provinces about their relationship with the federal government, the American "manifest destiny" movement that promoted annexation of Canada, the need to build a transportation system stretching from coast to coast as well as to populate the Prairies, and, more recently, the Quebec separatist movement, and undue influence over the Canadian economy by powerful American and multinational conglomerates and wealthy elites. As well, it was not until the country was well into its second century of existence that the Constitution was finally "brought home" from Britain, allowing Canadians full control over their own constitutional affairs.

Some people think the Canadian miracle may come to an end in the twenty-first century. They contend that Canada has become so dependent on the United States—economically, politically, militarily, and culturally—that it will, at best, soon exist in name only, lacking the ability to determine its own policies, directions, or destiny. Others contend that Canada's identity will be subsumed within a vast North and South American trade zone dominated by the United States, although resistance to such arrangements both in the U.S. and elsewhere in the Americas makes this prospect less likely than it once was.

The naysayers aside, however, most Canadians believe that Canada will not only remain independent but will go on to achieve bigger and better things. This might include a greater measure of independence from the United States, providing leadership to a troubled world, contributing in a major way to the welfare and well-being of people and countries elsewhere in the world, and, in sum, realizing the country's full potential and ultimate destiny.

As we consider these differing views and opinions, it is essential to take a long, hard look at how Canada came into existence, as well as the challenges and opportunities Canadians have faced over the centuries. In the process, we will find there is a great deal to be learned from the country's past that is relevant to its present and future development, as well as learning why the survival and well-being of Canada as a strong, independent country is a categorical imperative.

As I mentioned at the start of this chapter, the mere thought of creating a country in the northern half of the North American continent at one time seemed utterly impossible. All the major geographic arteries in North America—the Appalachian and Allegheny mountains in the east, the Rockies in the west, and many of the continent's most important waterways, including the Mississippi River—run north and south. This fact, together with the existence of the rugged and almost impenetrable Precambrian Shield in the far north, seemed to negate the possibility of creating a country stretching thousands of kilometres from the Atlantic Ocean in the east to the Pacific Ocean in the west and the Arctic Ocean in the north.

Canada's history began thousands of years ago with the arrival of the Indigenous peoples, who travelled across the land-bridge then connecting Siberia to North America and then moved progressively southward and eastward, looking for food and shelter and leaving behind pockets of population wherever feasible and desirable. Many of these peoples worked their way south to warmer climes, ultimately settling throughout most parts of Canada and the United States and also establishing the great Mayan, Aztec, and Incan civilizations of Central and South America.

Others, perhaps with a greater desire for adventure, pushed north or northeast into the demanding terrains and frigid temperatures of those regions and established permanent settlements there. Wherever they went, these inventive peoples created patterns of possibility and settlement that laid the foundations for the creation of Canada as, first and foremost, a northern country. This "northerness" has resided at the core of Canada's development and character for centuries and remains today. In following the call of these vital and various paths, the Indigenous peoples established a west-to-east and north-to-south pattern of habitation that defied the dictates and contours of North American geography, putting later generations of Canadians forever in their debt.

Centuries later, explorers from Europe began to arrive on the east coast and penetrate into the country's interior, moving in the opposite direction from the Indigenous peoples—from east to west and south to north, rather than the reverse. The Vikings (or Norse) arrived first. They travelled from Iceland and Greenland across the Atlantic around 1000 A.D. to establish the first European settlement in Canada at L'Anse aux Meadows on the northern tip of Newfoundland. Made up of three groups of stone buildings covered with turf and surrounded by a wooden barricade, it is today a UNESCO World Heritage site.

Later, explorers and fishermen began to arrive in substantial numbers along the North American seaboard, first from Spain and Portugal and later France and England. They took advantage of the abundant fisheries of the Grand Banks off the coast of what are now the Atlantic provinces. While the French used the "green" method of salting and curing fish on board their boats, thus not requiring settlements on land, the English used the "dry" method that did necessitate some permanent settlements. As revenue from the fishing industry increased due to the high demand for fish in Europe and incredible size of the fish stocks on the Grand Banks, France and England began to take a stronger interest in North America. The prospect of a western trade route to China also lured Europeans onward.

In 1497, England's Henry VII financed a voyage across the Atlantic Ocean by John Cabot that led to the "rediscovery" of Newfoundland, which had been abandoned by the Vikings during the Middle Ages. In response to this English initiative, the French monarchy financed three voyages by Jacques Cartier in 1534, 1535–36, and 1541. The first voyage saw further exploration of Newfoundland and Labrador, the second and third voyages exploration of the lower reaches of the St. Lawrence River and the area around present-day Quebec City and Montreal. Cartier called the area around Quebec and Montreal "Canada"—a word used by the Indigenous peoples to describe this particular region—and claimed it for France. His activities generated a great deal of interest in Europe, largely because he kept detailed accounts of the many different plants, animals, land forms, and people he encountered.

In 1600, the French crown granted a royal monopoly to explore and settle this "new-found-land." The first French colony of any size and significance was established at Port Royal on the Annapolis Basin in what is now Nova Scotia. When the colony proved impossible to sustain because of the risks and dangers involved as well as an inability to attract enough settlers, it was relocated to Quebec, whose name was derived from an Indigenous word meaning "where the river (i.e., the St. Lawrence) narrows." The person who led this relocation was Samuel de Champlain, who turned out to be one of Canada's most formidable and visionary leaders. Not only did he and his troops explore most of the land up and down the St. Lawrence River and as far west as Georgian Bay in Ontario, meticulously mapping much of what they discovered along the way, but they also played a key role in making contact with the Indigenous peoples and conducting trade with them, especially in furs. As it turned out, these relations were beneficial to both the Europeans and the First Nations, as H. V. Nelles points out in his book *A Little History of Canada*:

> The survival of this emerging colony [Quebec] required adaptation by the French to a North American environment and by the indigenous peoples to the presence of the French. Through contact, the two cultures developed mutual respect—and, it must be said, reciprocal animosity. The French borrowed indigenous technologies—canoes, snowshoes, and toboggans—to travel in the new landscape, adopted some aspects of Native clothing, and had recourse to herbal remedies for sickness and injuries. Native peoples coveted European knives, textiles, utensils, and weapons.*

---

* H.V. Nelles, *A Little History of Canada* (Toronto: Oxford University Press, 2004), p. 27.

As the interaction between the French and English increased both in Europe and North America, competition intensified. The French put a great deal of effort, energy, and money into reinforcing the colony at what is now Quebec City since it occupied a position of strategic importance. The decision by King Louis XIV in 1663 to revoke the charter given to the Company of the Hundred Associates and make the colony at Quebec—or New France as it was called—a "royal province" with the same status as a province in France did more than anything else to establish a strong, permanent, and aggressive French presence in Canada, and had a fundamental bearing on all that has taken place in Canada since then. The Quebec colony was governed by a superior or sovereign council appointed by the king. The governor was responsible for the colony in general and military and external affairs in particular, an intendant for internal matters and administration, and a bishop for religious matters. From the 1660s to the 1680s, these three posts were held by Frontenac, Jean-Baptiste Talon, and Bishop Laval respectively who together transformed the colony from a small, weak, fragile, and largely missionary outpost into a prosperous, populous, and highly productive royal province. They accomplished this feat by taking full advantage of the fish, fur, timber, and minerals to be found in the area, encouraging commercial farming, promoting shipbuilding, and exporting wood, wool, hemp, hides, barley, hops, and tar to France, the West Indies, and other destinations. Under the leadership of this powerful triumvirate, the colony of New France became a force to be reckoned with.

By the time the Quebec colony was asserting its power and influence, the fur trade was starting to replace the fishery industry as the most important and lucrative economic activity. The fur trade was destined to drive the next phase in the creation of Canada. Unlike fishing, it necessitated deep penetration into the country's interior. It also heightened the bitter rivalry between French and English in North America and in Europe.

By the middle of the eighteenth century, these two great European nations dominated the development of the fur trade in what was to become Canada a century later. The "French system," centred on the St. Lawrence River and the Great Lakes, was predicated on developing the North West Company with its headquarters in Montreal. Fully developed, the company's reach extended from Montreal to the upper reaches of the Mississippi River and its northern tributaries, as well as to the Prairies and the southern parts of the Canadian Shield. The "English system," whose centrepiece was the Hudson's Bay Company, the first and today the oldest commercial company in North America, took as its preserve what was called Rupert's Land, the entire region draining into Hudson Bay and James Bay, extending to the Arctic Ocean in the north and the Pacific Ocean in the west.

Whereas the development of the fishing industry encouraged activity and settlement along the two "book-ends" of Canada—namely the east and west coasts—the fur trade generated development and settlement across the entire length and breadth of the country. The evolution of these two "staples industries" was described in great detail by one of the country's most respected economic historians, Harold Innis, in two of the most important books ever written on the early development of Canada, *The Fur Trade in Canada* and *The Cod Fisheries: History of an International Economy*.

What made the fur trade so important to the creation of Canada as a country was the fact it required the establishment of forts, trading posts, and settlements at strategic locations across the continent. It led to the reconnaissance of much of North America by such hardy explorers as Pierre-Esprit Raddison, Médard des Grosseillers, Martin Frobisher, Robert de La Salle, Jacques Marquette, Louis Joliett, Samuel Hearne, Simon Fraser, David Thompson, Alexander Mackenzie, John Franklin, and many others.

Most of these explorers were born in France, England, or elsewhere in Europe. They kept detailed records and mapped large areas of North America. Two of the most important and respected were David Thompson and Alexander Mackenzie. Thompson, who was known to the Indigenous peoples as "Koo-Koo-Sint" or "the stargazer," was deemed by some to be "the greatest land geographer who ever lived" since he mapped almost four million square kilometres of North America. Mackenzie, in 1793 the first European to travel overland to the Pacific Ocean, accomplished this feat ten years before the famous American expedition to the Pacific led by Lewis and Clark. These explorations by Mackenzie, Thompson, and many others did a great deal to open up the interior of Canada. Without them, Canada would likely not have come into existence until much later, and presumably in a very different form.

While these developments occurred in the west and north, things were heating up in the east. The conflict between Britain and France in Europe was spilling over to the other side of the Atlantic, especially in what are now Nova Scotia, Quebec, and southern Ontario. While France had controlled most of this territory from the creation of New France until the 1730s and '40s, Britain was determined to bring French domination to an end. Large numbers of troops and settlers were dispatched to eastern Canada in general and Nova Scotia and Halifax in particular, where a major colony meant to offset the power of the French colony at Louisburg was established. France's position in North America was threatened.

Matters came to a head during the Seven Years' War from 1754 to 1763. The war involved numerous countries in Europe, but at its core was a struggle between France and Britain. In the end, the British were successful in overcoming the French in Europe as well as in North America. Louisbourg fell in 1758, Quebec was captured in 1759—following a famous battle in which the British (led by James Wolfe) defeated the French (led by the Marquis de Montcalm) by ingeniously scaling the cliffs above the St. Lawrence River at Quebec at night and prevailing on the Plains of Abraham the next day—and Montreal was taken in 1760. The Treaty of Paris of 1763 saw France cede virtually all its lands and colonies in what later became Canada to Britain. The treaty also paved the way for major changes in other parts of North America, which was by then almost exclusively under British control.

In order to govern this vast area, the British had to work out arrangements with the Indigenous peoples—some tribes had supported the French and others the English—as well as the French-speaking population in Quebec and other parts of North America.

The Royal Proclamation of 1763, issued by George III, established the foundations for British administration in North America and created an overarching framework for negotiation of treaties with the First Nations. The proclamation became known as the "Indian Magna Carta" or "Indian Bill of Rights" because it addressed not only the rights of the country's Indigenous peoples but also ceded a vast section of the North American interior west of the Appalachians to these peoples as a huge reserve.

The proclamation was viewed in Quebec largely as a vehicle for assimilating the French-speaking settlers as well as the Indigenous peoples into the British mode of governance and overall way of life. It was followed by the Quebec Act in 1774. Not only did this act annex the Ohio region to Canada for administrative purposes, bringing the commerce of the western interior back under the control of the governor in Quebec, but also it set out procedures for the governance of Quebec and the French population generally. It defined the geographic area encompassed by

Quebec, guaranteed protection of the Catholic faith, instituted a joint regime of English criminal and French civil law, provided for an appointed legislative council which included Roman Catholics, and re-established the Catholic Church's right to impose and collect tithes.

While the Quebec Act accomplished a great deal in terms of facilitating future relations between the French and English in Canada—relations based largely on integration and cooperation rather than assimilation and oppression—it produced a strong backlash and much hostility among the largely Protestant and English inhabitants of the thirteen American colonies, primarily because it imposed constraints on the independence of the colonial legislatures, prevented territorial expansion, interfered with the colonies' freedom to trade, and levied taxes without representation.

As a result, the Quebec Act was numbered among the so-called "Intolerable Acts" (along with other grievances) that caused the American colonies to revolt against Britain, issuing the Declaration of Independence on July 4, 1776. The American colonists invited Quebec to join the revolution, but clerical and administrative leaders in Quebec declined to place their trust in a future nation they felt would not respect their laws, language, culture, and religious beliefs. An invasion of what eventually became Canada had to be driven back by a small force that surprisingly included French militia as well as Indigenous tribes.

By 1783 the British acknowledged they had lost the war and the independence of the United States was secured. Some 60,000 colonists who had sided with the British government and now found themselves on the losing side emigrated to Canada. These United Empire Loyalists settled in what are now Nova Scotia, New Brunswick, and Ontario.

For their part, the British concluded that there were important lessons to be learned from the American Revolution. As H. V. Nelles points out, the British decided that their remaining colonies in North America had to be

> endowed with a constitution and social make-up resembling that of Britain itself. Having lost the first empire, the British were determined not to lose the second. The Constitution Act of 1791 created two colonies, Upper Canada and Lower Canada, each with its own administration and Legislative Assembly. In Upper Canada, British laws and institutions would prevail. In Lower Canada, a mixed system of English criminal law, common law, and French civil

law would continue; seigniorial tenure would apply to most of the province and an English freehold system would govern in the newly settled townships.[*]

As these developments were taking place, and sensing that the British were too preoccupied with the Napoleonic Wars in Europe to pay much attention to North America, the U.S. government felt the time had come to extend its territory. With the Maritimes protected by British sea power and Lower Canada by the strong colony and fortress at Quebec, the "softest" target for the United States was Upper Canada, now Ontario. As Arthur Lower points out, "The War of 1812 . . . was the first of many American efforts at western expansion by armed force." This North American war was clearly a minor counterpoint to the conflict raging in Europe, but in Canada it produced invasions directed at the capture of Kingston, Niagara, York (Toronto), and the Detroit River in addition to Montreal and Quebec.

The population of the United States by this point was many times greater than that of the British colonies in North America. Though not all Americans supported the war, at the same time there was little confidence in London that English and French Canadians were anxious to die in a European-dominated war that seemed to hold little relevance to their daily lives. However, in the battle at Queenston Heights, British troops, Canadian militia, and a variety of Indigenous tribes defeated the much larger American army. It was a remarkable victory. The brave and intelligent General Isaac Brock, who together with the wise Shawnee Chief Tecumseh whose indispensable contribution to the war after Brock's death has never been properly recognized, emerged as the man who saved Canada from the American invasion. Interestingly, Brock is the only military hero Canada has ever really embraced. This is in stark contrast to the large array of military heroes such as Washington, Grant, Lee, Patton, McArthur, and Eisenhower who grace the history books of United States.

As insignificant as it may seem in the global context, the War of 1812 has often been called Canada's "War of Independence," with all the significance this designation suggests. It affirmed Canada's continuing presence in the upper half of the North American continent.

Unfortunately, the War of 1812 did not put an end to the unfriendly relations between the U.S. and British North America. Rebellions in

[*] Nelles, *Little History*, p. 81.

Ontario and Quebec in 1837–38 led some Americans to believe many still under British rule wanted to become citizens of the United States. As a result, organizations of aggressive American citizens called Hunters' Lodges took it upon themselves to make incursions into Canadian territory until it became clear that Canadians were not rebelling against British rule as such, but, rather, against power-hungry oligarchies like the Family Compact in Upper Canada and the Parti Patriote in Lower Canada— oligarchies that were misusing their power and needed to be replaced by more democratic institutions and procedures.

Meanwhile, tension remained between the French and English in Canada. Discouraged, the British government dispatched Lord Durham to North America in 1838 to investigate the situation in the wake of the unsuccessful rebellions. His report, the famous "Durham Report" of the schoolbooks, proposed the union of all the British colonies in North America and the implementation of "responsible" (i.e., democratic) government.

The proposed comprehensive union was not accepted, largely because of the objections of Nova Scotia and New Brunswick. However, the Report did begin the process of bringing together (in Durham's words) "two nations warring in the bosom of a single state" through the Act of Union, proclaimed in 1841, which saw Upper Canada and Lower Canada combined into one "Province of Canada." The province was divided into Canada East and Canada West, with equal representation for each. Louis Lafontaine in Canada East and Robert Baldwin in Canada West overcame numerous obstacles to make the union work for the benefit of all.

The War of 1812, the Durham Report, and the fur trade all contributed substantially to the creation of Canada as a country. In fact, Harold Innis called the fur trade *the* defining factor in the country's development:

> Canada emerged as a political entity with boundaries largely determined by the fur trade. These boundaries included a vast north temperate land area extending from the Atlantic to the Pacific. *The present Dominion emerged not in spite of geography but because of it. The significance of the fur trade consisted in its determination of the geographic framework.**

---

* Harold A. Innis, *The Fur Trade in Canada*, p. 393.

Another force, however, was gathering momentum, one which was also destined to play a major role in the creation of Canada as an independent country. Ironically, this was the "manifest destiny" movement in the United States, a movement that called for the annexation of Canada. It quickly became a standard part of the political vocabulary of American presidential candidates. Simply put, it was based on the belief that the United States had a "God-given right" to extend its control over all of North America by persuasion, coercion, or force if necessary. As one American politician put it: "I hope to see the day when the American flag will float over every square foot of the British North American possessions clear to the North Pole."

This concept, which reached its zenith in the second half of the nineteenth century but remained influential into the early years of the twentieth century, became the justification for almost every expansionary action on the part of the United States, from the conquest of Texas, New Mexico, and California in the south to the expectation that the lands held by the Hudson's Bay Company in the northwestern reaches of the continent would eventually fall into American hands.

Canadians were fully aware of the threat posed by the movement. This concern was evident in the 1850s and '60s. For a time, the U.S. Civil War diverted American attention from the empty, undefended western and northern lands that would eventually be an integral part of Canada. However, it was clear by 1864 that the North would be victorious in its war with the South, and would therefore dominate the political life of the republic. A massive army now existed that, when the war ended, could be used, if so desired, to fulfill the dreams of manifest destiny, while at the same time Britain was anxious to reduce its military presence and financial expenditures in British North America. For the British, the North American colonies had become too expensive to administer, too costly to defend, too irksome, troublesome, and quarrelsome. As Benjamin Disraeli said in a speech to the British Parliament, "These wretched colonies will all be independent too, in a few years, and are a millstone around our necks."[*]

John A. Macdonald, who by the mid-1860s had become the preeminent political figure in the Canadas, had no illusions about being able to depend on Britain for defence if the U.S. turned its sights northward. The time was ripe to establish Canada as a country. This was accomplished

---

[*] Nelles, *Little History of Canada,* p. 116.

through the passage of the British North America Act by the British Parliament in 1867, leading to the creation of the Dominion of Canada on July 1 of that same year. Four British colonies—Nova Scotia, New Brunswick, Quebec, and Ontario—became the founding provinces. The new dominion—the term was derived from Psalm 72, which states "[H]e shall have dominion from sea to sea"—was intended from the start as a federal *state* rather than a confederation of associated *states*, and was meant to avoid the issue of states' rights that had led to the Civil War. Interestingly, Canada's act of union was predicated on "peace, order, and good government," whereas America's proclaimed the importance of "life, liberty, and the pursuit of happiness." This contrast was to have major implications for Canada in the years following Confederation.

Confederation was an initiative driven by Canadian citizens and their various governments through a series of conferences that hammered out in great detail the kind of country they wanted to have. They did so with great alacrity, fearing that invasion from the south could occur at any time. Their fears concerning more invasions were not unfounded, and were confirmed when a group of British-hating Irish Americans founded a military organization called the Fenians and launched a series of raids on Canada West, in the process encouraging the movement toward Confederation. The colonial status of the country demanded that the BNA Act be a *British* act of Parliament. However, it was "made in Canada" in every other respect.

While Confederation was a gigantic step forward, numerous problems and pressures continued to threaten the continued existence and independence of the country. What was most needed was an intercontinental railway to link all parts of the country together, the creation of an economic and industrial policy that would strengthen the ties binding the new nation together, and the settlement of the west to forestall American expansion.

Working at a feverish pitch, the Canadian Pacific Railway (CPR) was completed by 1881, both through the incorporation of lines already built in the east and the construction of a great deal of new track in the west under exceedingly difficult geographic conditions, including countless bogs and insect-infested swamps, challenging mountainous terrain, and surging rivers. The CPR was built to extend Canada from coast to coast and fulfill a promise made to British Columbia to convince it to join Confederation, which it did in 1871. The western part of the CPR was built largely with British, American, and Canadian capital, as well as a great deal of Chinese labour, and was one of the greatest engineering feats in human history. Indeed, Canada may be the only country in the world that was created and sustained for a long period by transportation technology. Railways provided the glue that held Canada together for many decades.

Devising a plan to tie the new country together economically and industrially was also imperative. Unless alternatives were provided, western Canadians would buy their farm machinery from suppliers in North Dakota and eastern Canadians would buy agricultural and consumer goods from nearby American states. The most effective way to prevent this from happening was to create a tariff barrier that encouraged industrial development in Canada while simultaneously keeping foreign and especially American manufactured goods out. This was the principal objective behind John A. Macdonald's "National Policy," although these tariffs were resented by many Canadians anxious to buy cheaper goods in the United States.

Nonetheless, the early industrialization of Canada came from the realization that survival alongside the rapidly evolving American industrial giant was possible only through the development of a strong, dynamic, and viable *Canadian* economy. Without economic unity and independence predicated on conscious and consistent governmental policies, the pressure of American political and corporate power might easily end Canada's great adventure before it had barely begun.

A rebellion around this time also threatened the continued existence of the country and had to be quelled. This was the Riel Rebellion in the west. It was caused by the sudden transfer of authority by London of the Hudson's Bay Company and its lands to the Canadian government without any consultation with local people and communities. This insensitive policy led to disruptions in land use and ownership, commerce, and agriculture among the Red River settlers in the west, who were called Métis and were largely of French-Indigenous extraction. Also contributing was pressure from Americans who felt that great profits could be had from the sale of land and control of the fur trade in what was to become the hurriedly created Province of Manitoba. While peace was eventually restored, it came at a severe price. Louis Riel was hanged in 1885, an event which produced strong reactions among the Métis in the west and most French Canadians in the east.

Yet another development around this time touched upon the continued and fragile existence of Canada as a country. While the east was rapidly filling up with people and gathering momentum industrially and commercially, in large measure as a result of the timber trade, which had replaced the fur trade as the driving economic force, the west remained almost devoid of settlers. A policy was quickly devised to "fill up the west" with immigrants from Europe and other parts of the world.

In 1896, Wilfrid Laurier was elected prime minister and promptly appointed Clifford Sifton as his interior minister with responsibility for implementing an urgently required immigration and settlement policy. By 1905, 22.5 million of the 24 million acres of land promised to the railways were made available to immigrants and settlers under extremely favourable financial conditions by the federal government. The plan was to fill Manitoba, as well as Saskatchewan and Alberta, which had just joined Confederation, with farms and farmers. This would turn the prairies into a huge agricultural area capable of producing wheat and other grains that would complement the industrial region being developed in the east, as well as capitalize on the recently established CPR to facilitate trade and communication between the western and eastern parts of the country.

Even after Confederation and the securing of Canada's border with the United States, however, independence was not fully assured. Canada was still a colony of Britain in most ways. The British government continued to appoint Canada's Governors General; Britain still conducted most of the country's international affairs; and the final court of appeal was a committee of the House of Lords in London—the Judicial Committee of the Privy Council—rather than the Supreme Court of Canada.

Things started to change and change significantly in this area during and after the First World War. This was due to the performance of Canadian troops at Vimy Ridge, Passchendaele, and especially during the "last hundred days" when Canada became a "country in its own right" in the eyes of many people. This led to a separate signing by Canada of the Treaty of Versailles after the war.

Not long after the end of the First World War, another development occurred that posed a serious threat to Canada's independent existence. While it was not as serious as the earlier manifest destiny movement in the United States—let's be clear on this point—it also came from south of the border and threatened to make Canada more dependent on foreign rather than domestic sources of information and ideas. Strange as it may sound, the new threat was the advent of radio in the 1920s and '30s. High-power U.S. radio stations pumped American news, ideas, and information into Canada and some Canadian stations joined the fledgling U.S. networks. Was this a new phase in the manifest destiny movement and Canada's evolving relations with the United States?

As before, Canada responded to this development with alarm and haste. It created the Canadian Broadcasting Corporation (CBC) in 1936, following a period of intense lobbying by the Canadian Radio League, the passage of the Radio Act of 1927, and the establishment of the Royal Commission on Radio (the Aird Commission) in 1928.

The CBC was created to "develop a national broadcasting service for all Canadians in both official languages, which would be primarily Canadian in content and character." The decision to create it was an historic one that has had a profound effect on Canadian development ever since. For one thing, it was a remarkable engineering feat, since a grid of capital facilities had to be created across the country that made it possible to disseminate Canadian news, information, ideas, and programs from the Atlantic to the Pacific and into the far north. For another, it indicated that the federal government was committed to combating American cultural penetration into Canada by encouraging domestic activity rather than impeding foreign activity, a course of action which, with few exceptions, has been followed in Canada to this day by all levels of government. Finally, it demonstrated a preference for dealing with complex administrative problems in the field of broadcasting and communications by creating autonomous agencies operating at arm's length from government and the political process, rather than direct involvement on the part of government departments and ministries.

It wasn't long before the CBC was recognized as a genuine Canadian icon. Not only did it play a key role in linking the country and its citizenry together from coast to coast to coast, but it provided economic and artistic opportunities to talented Canadians to produce a vast variety of dynamic and diversified programs, thereby substantially expanding Canadian content. The CBC also played a crucial role in keeping Canadians informed about Canada's remarkable accomplishments during the Second World War.

By the war's end, Canada had become a major industrial power. There were those, however, among the country's corporate elite who favoured the sale of the country's natural resources and even some of its industrial assets to foreign (usually American) companies. With the Cold War just getting underway, it was seen as patriotic to follow a capitalist, laissez-faire philosophy that had little regard for national boundaries or political priorities. As long as there was full employment and significant increases in material well-being, there was little discussion of the fact that, at its roots, such a policy was designed primarily to enrich the powerful and the wealthy. Once again, the existence of the country was being tested and even called into question.

Here too, there were people who sounded the alarm. One was Harold Innis, who was mentioned earlier. He was especially concerned about what he called "the staples trap"—too much dependence on natural resources (i.e., "staples") and too little industrial development. Such an overreliance would, he felt, undermine Canada's independence. Also concerned was George Grant. His *Lament for a Nation* (1965) was popular with many Canadians because it saw in the defeat of Prime Minister John Diefenbaker the disappearance of the last opportunity to save the country. The Conservative Party of this period recalled the legacy of John A. Macdonald and his National Policy, while the Liberals, in contrast, were more continentalist, prepared to bend (though not break) in the face of American economic might. However, it was a Liberal, Walter Gordon, who became the hero of Canadian nationalists in the 1960s. Appointed Finance Minister under Liberal Prime Minister Lester Pearson, he was often viewed as the sole cabinet member determined to keep Canada together and independent from the United States.

Gordon was so appalled by the lack of commitment to Canada's continued independence by his cabinet colleagues that in 1968 he appointed Mel Watkins, an economist from the University of Toronto, to examine the extent of American domination of the Canadian economy. Watkins concluded that without government action to prevent it, control of the Canadian economy would slip into the hands of American corporations, with Canada becoming a kind of branch plant or resource colony of the United States. By 1971, over 76% of Canadian business enterprises with assets over $25 million were in foreign hands, the large majority owned by Americans.

Could a country that surrendered this much power, influence, and control over its corporate and industrial affairs to another country still be considered independent? Was Canada in danger of becoming a colony of the United States, so soon after it had laboured to divest itself of British colonial status?

Canada faced other problems after the Second World War apart from foreign domination of the economy. The rise of Quebec nationalism and separatism in the 1950s and '60's was seen by many in that province as a response to the lack of commitment in English-speaking Canada to remaining a sovereign and independent country. With the advent of a more global approach to economic development, many French-speaking Québécois concluded that they could form a viable and exciting economic, political, and cultural entity of their own that would incorporate the best features of nationhood. In their eyes, the English-led continentalism that was undermining Canada's independence would ultimately result in the destruction of a country that had for so long respected French language, culture, and traditions.

There was certainly a real distrust of *les anglais* who dominated corporations and financial institutions in Quebec, but there was even less hope for the survival of the "French fact" in a Canada that was a colony or branch plant of the United States. It was no small triumph that although these decades were obsessed with efforts to contain French-Canadian outrage and encourage English Canadians to accept Quebec and French realities, there was comparatively little violence and at no time a cessation of the determination of most Canadians to keep the country together.

During the 1970s, '80's, and '90's, strong pressures were exerted for Quebec to become an independent nation, particularly after the election of the Parti Québécois under the charismatic leadership of René Lévesque. This situation became explosive when attempts were made to patriate the country's constitution by the Liberal Government of Pierre Elliott Trudeau. While such attempts had been ongoing since the 1920s, the re-election of the Trudeau government seemed to provide an ideal time to fulfill this dream. This ultimately led in 1982 to the transfer of Canada's highest law, the British North America Acts (which included the original act of 1867 and subsequent amendments) from the authority of the British Parliament to Canada's federal and provincial legislatures. The new constitution included an amending formula and the Canadian Charter of Rights and Freedoms.

Regrettably, Quebec was not included in this historic initiative because it did not agree with the changes made in the Constitution Act and especially with how the patriation process was conducted. Attempts were then made by a Conservative government under Brian Mulroney to "bring Quebec into the constitutional family" through the Meech Lake Accord of 1987. When this process also failed, yet another effort was made to close the rift between Quebec and the rest of Canada through the 1992 Charlottetown Accord, which recognized Quebec's distinct language and culture and transferred authority over mining, forestry, telecommunications, and other areas to the provinces.

When a national referendum was held on the Charlottetown Accord, it was rejected by a majority of Canadians, further aggravating the situation. A second independence referendum in Quebec was defeated by an even narrower margin than the first (49.7% to 48.5% with 1.8% of ballots spoiled), primarily because of last-minute interventions by the federal government and a real show of affection by Canadians from other provinces, including a major rally in Montreal.

Many felt that had the referendum succeeded, Canada's very existence as a country would have been in doubt, especially as some of the other provinces indicated they might think seriously about joining the United States if Quebec seceded. Fortunately this worst-case scenario did not come to pass, and the passage of the Clarity Act in 2000 changed the entire dynamic, since it required in future referenda a clear and unambiguous question as to whether Quebecers wanted to remain in Canada or leave it.

Despite how painful this process was at the time, it proved to be a beneficial experience for Canadians. People living outside Quebec became much more aware of how important it is for Quebec to preserve its language, culture, identity, status as a nation, and way of life, how essential this is for the continued existence of Canada as a country, and why it is so imperative for Quebec to have control over the political and administrative means that are required to develop and cultivate these cultural necessities in Canada as well as in La Francophonie and other parts of the world in the years and decades ahead. But the people of Quebec also gained something of crucial importance. They learned that countless people in other parts of Canada are deeply committed to Quebec's sustained existence in the country, cherish the many valuable contributions Quebec and Quebeckers have made and are making to Canadian development, and want them to stay in Canada rather than leave it.

One other development of the late twentieth and early twenty-first century should be mentioned—the free trade movement. While it didn't threaten the continued existence of Canada as such, it did threaten Canada's economic independence from the United States. Although free trade with the United States was not discussed prior to the 1984 election, Brian Mulroney, the new Conservative prime minister, wasted no time in bringing this matter to national attention. In spite of the general well-being of the country, there was an apocalyptic sense about the subject of free trade. To turn down free trade with the United States was to court disaster in the minds of many Canadians, especially business and political leaders, while in their view free trade promised greater prosperity. After heated debate, a free trade agreement with the United States was signed in 1988. This was subsumed in the North American Free Trade Agreement (NAFTA) in 1994 when Mexico joined the pact. While this arrangement has produced many benefits for citizens of all three countries, it has not been without its problems. Not only did it result in a further hollowing out of the Canadian economy with the loss of manufacturing jobs and capabilities, but it also pushed Canada even further toward becoming a U.S. branch plant. Once more, the spectre of Innis's "staples trap" aroused the concern of many Canadians. These fears were rekindled by the signing of the Canadian-European Trade Agreement (CETA) in 2016.

After overcoming numerous threats to the country's continued existence in the century and a half since Confederation, Canadians now find themselves in the position of having to decide how much loss of control over industry and what degree of dependence on natural resources is tolerable. This decision must be based on more than simply a fear that Canada will be drawn even more fully into the American empire in the future. It will also have to be grounded in something other than a feeling that the country's independence is constantly being challenged or at risk.

On the contrary, it will have to be part of a rapidly evolving realization that Canada's remarkable battle to become and remain a distinct and independent country against virtually insurmountable odds, as well as its ability to create a superb quality of life for most of its citizens, place the country in an ideal position to strike out in a bold new direction in the future. This means becoming masters in our own home and shapers of our own destiny, with full control over our domestic and international affairs. For what this chapter's review of Canadian history has revealed is that Canada possesses all the capabilities and attributes required to achieve this and provide leadership to a troubled world.

The country and its people have always defied the odds. There is now ample evidence to suggest Canada will not only continue to exist but will go on to achieve even bigger and better things. Canadians possess all they need to overcome the obstacles that stand in their way and play an exemplary role in the world. Without doubt, this is Canada's destiny in the remaining decades of the twenty-first century.

CHAPTER THREE

Creativity Is the Key

T here is an image of Pierre Elliott Trudeau indelibly etched on the minds of many Canadians. It is the image of Trudeau in a buckskin jacket, paddling a canoe somewhere on a lake in northern Canada.

What makes this image so powerful is not only the fact that Trudeau was one of Canada's most respected and charismatic political leaders, but also that the canoe played a crucial role in the development of Canada. The canoe made it possible to come to grips with a whole series of formidable economic, geographic, and transportation challenges. Small wonder that authorities at the Canadian Canoe Museum in Peterborough contend that "the canoe is a Canadian icon.... Canada exists because of the canoe. The canoe determined national boundaries and carried sovereignty to the northern half of the continent."

While Canadians did not invent the canoe, they made many important refinements to it, and actually did invent the *birchbark* canoe. As important as the canoe was (and is), it represents only a tiny fraction of the creativity for which Canadians have been responsible over the centuries.* Creative Canadian inventions and innovations include the telephone, kerosene, the snowmobile, the wire-photo transmitter, standard time, Marquis wheat, walkie-talkies, frozen fish fillets for commercial use, various aspects of petrochemical refining and map-making, the production of paper from pulp wood, applications of automation to industrial processes, the fog horn, the variable pitch propeller, insulin, Pablum, the cardiac pacemaker, ice hockey, basketball, lacrosse, the BlackBerry, and many others. The degree of creativity demonstrated by Canadians should come as no surprise; Canadians have been compelled to be creative in

---

* Canadian creativity is examined in detail in my book *Celebrating Canadian Creativity* (revised Canada 150 edition, Rock's Mills Press, 2017).

order to survive, prosper, create a dynamic and progressive economy, and come to grips with the country's numerous challenges.

Not surprisingly, creativity has followed the general contours of Canadian development over the centuries. In earlier centuries, it was usually channelled into the basics—food, clothing, and shelter—as well as the construction of an effective transportation and communication system. While creativity has continued to pour forth in all these areas, over the last century or so it has also been channelled into producing higher standards of living and a better quality of life for the country's citizens, and has expressed itself in fields as diverse as agriculture, industry, education, politics, health and welfare, science, technology, the arts, recreation, sports, and the environment.

We are speaking here of creativity in a broad, generic sense. As such, it includes inventions, innovations, what Northrop Frye meant when he used the term "the imagination," and what Homer Dixon means when he uses the term "ingenuity." It is everything that springs from the need to do things in unique and original ways, create things that do not exist, solve complex problems, overcome difficulties, and take advantage of new opportunities. It is a seamless web that manifests itself in virtually every dimension of Canadian life.

Viewed in this way, creativity is without doubt Canada's most valuable asset. The country's survival was, is, and always will be heavily dependent on it. However, and more to the point as far as this book is concerned, Canadian creativity is imperative if Canada and Canadians are to make the contributions of which they are capable to the development of the country and the world at large.

For hundreds of years prior to the arrival of the first Europeans, the Indigenous peoples responded to the challenges of what eventually became Canada in highly original and unique ways. In the process, they developed many processes, practices, and inventions that proved useful to the generations of European settlers who followed in their footsteps. Most of this creativity was channelled into areas that were of crucial importance for survival, especially agriculture, transportation, and communications. For instance, the transportation networks created by the Hudson's Bay Company and the North West Company made it possible to link sparse pockets of population together and for fur traders, trappers, and explorers to penetrate deep into the interior of the continent.

Building on these foundations, Canadians are recognized as world leaders in the development of transportation technology and systems today. It is not difficult to draft a long list of creative Canadian achievements in the field: the construction of the Rideau and Welland canals and the St. Lawrence Seaway; creation of the first transatlantic steamship, the *Royal William*, as well as a workable screw propeller by Joseph Patch of Nova Scotia; construction of two of the longest railroads in the world, the CPR and, later, the Canadian National Railway (CNR); the first powered flight in the British Empire (the Silver Dart, piloted by J.A.D. McCurdy in 1909); and the invention of the variable pitch propeller by W.R. Turnbull in 1922, making it possible for airplanes to carry larger and therefore more economically viable payloads and opening the way for the development of commercial aviation.

To this list should be added construction of the first commercial jetliner, the C-102 Avro Jetliner as well as the innovative jet fighter the Avro Arrow, the invention of the snowmobile by Joseph-Armand Bombardier, and a string of successful innovations in small plane technology, such as the Dash-7 and Dash-8 designed and built by DeHavilland Aircraft in Toronto, as well as the development of the bush plane for search and rescue missions in the north.

If Canada can lay claim to many creative achievements in transportation, it boasts a similar record in communications. In fact, Canadians have been at the cutting edge of creative developments in this area for more than two centuries, from communication by print and newspaper to communication by radio, television, film, photography, and mobile and wireless technology. Although these developments were often made in conjunction with people in other countries or by Canadians living and working elsewhere, many had the effect of creating new industries or transforming old ones, thereby substantially altering industrial, commercial, and economic practices around the world. As J.J. Brown, champion of Canadian creativity and ingenuity, pointed out in his book *The Inventors: Great Ideas in Canadian Enterprise*: "Whenever we pick up a phone, open a picture magazine, switch on the radio or send a telegram, we are in debt to a Canadian inventor. All these modern means of communication, each of which changed our world, would not have been possible without the inventive genius of men like Bell, Desbarats, Gisborne, Creed, Stevenson, and Rogers."

In the nineteenth century, important accomplishments in communications included the laying of the first Atlantic cable from Valentia, Ireland to Trinity Bay, Newfoundland in 1858 and the invention of the telephone by Alexander Graham Bell in Brantford in 1874. The creation of standard time zones by Sir Sandford Fleming in 1879 must also be mentioned. The string of innovations continued into the twentieth century, which opened with two very important developments: receiving the first transatlantic wireless signal by Guglielmo Marconi at Signal Hill, Newfoundland from Poldhu, near Cornwall, England, in 1901; and the laying of the first cable across the Pacific Ocean from Vancouver to Brisbane, Australia in 1902. In the 1920s, the wire photo transmitter was invented by Sir William Stephenson, who is better known as the master spy and subject of the book *A Man Called Intrepid* because of the role he played in coordinating British, American, and Canadian intelligence during the Second World War. Transmission of voices and visual images by Reginald Aubrey Fessenden in the early part of the twentieth century played a seminal role in the development of radio and later television broadcasting, as did creation of the batteryless radio by Edward Samuel (Ted) Rogers in 1927 and the establishment in 1920 of one of the first commercial radio stations in the world, CFCF ("Canada's First, Canada's Finest").

Thanks to these achievements in transportation and communications and the public institutions and agencies that grew out of them, Canadians were able to travel over long distances in ever shorter periods of time; families, friends, and relatives were able to stay in touch over long distances; and goods, information, ideas, and messages were transmitted and dispatched from coast to coast. The history of Canada would be very different without them.

It is easy to understand why Canadians have poured so much of their creativity into transportation and communication. The geographical dictates of the country, coupled with the need to transport people, products, information, and ideas over long distances in shorter and shorter periods of time, necessitated it. As Pierre Berton once said, "Canadians have made contributions to technology out of all proportion to their numbers."

With such historical precedents, it is likely no coincidence that two of the world's greatest communications theorists—Harold Innis and Marshall McLuhan—are Canadian. As communications expert Bruce Powe said, Canada was the first "electric nation" in the world and is first and foremost a "communications culture."

What is true of transportation and communications is also the case in many other fields. Since throughout its history Canada has generated its wealth largely through the development of natural resources and the extraction industries, creativity was applied to a whole host of innovative developments in agriculture, industry, fishing, forestry, mining, metallurgy, map-making, hydroelectricity, energy, and so forth. Canadian creativity runs the gamut of possibilities here, from producing better brands of wheat, barley, and cooking oil in Alberta, Saskatchewan, and Manitoba, to the harnessing of hydroelectric power in Ontario and Quebec, the creation of a national atlas, and the first commercial processing of fish through the development of frozen fish fillets by Archibald G. Huntsman in Nova Scotia.

As the nineteenth century drew to a close, agricultural creativity was essential. Canada needed crops that could withstand the country's long, cold winters and come to maturity in a short growing season. Answering this need was Marquis wheat, which was created by Charles Saunders in 1908. Prior to this time, the most common variety of wheat in Canada was Red Fife, which had been developed by David Fife in Ontario in 1875. While this strain served well in those parts of the country where the growing season was longer, it was not as suitable in the west because of the short growing season and early frosts. Capitalizing on research by his father, who was also extremely creative, Charles Saunders created Marquis wheat by crossing Red Fife with a south Asian variety called Red Calcutta. Since Marquis wheat matured in less time than Red Fife, produced significantly higher yields, and was more resistant to disease, it proved a bonanza for farmers in Canada and elsewhere. Within a few decades, farmers everywhere in the world where the growing season was shorter were dependent on the Canadian "miracle grain." Also vital to the growth and development of the Canadian prairies was Thomas Carroll's invention of the self-propelled combine harvester for the Massey-Harris company in 1937. This machine, able to cut, thresh, clean, and deliver grain in one operation, was a real spur to the production of wheat and other cereals in Canada and other parts of the world.

One might expect a country like Canada with large amounts of arable land to produce pioneering achievements in agriculture. However, it is more difficult to understand what led to highly creative achievements in industrial development in the later part of the nineteenth and early part of the twentieth century. Two of the most important of these were the discovery of kerosene by Abraham Gesner, and the timely contributions by Thomas Willson to the industrial use of acetylene and calcium carbide. These discoveries led to further strategic developments in petrochemical refining and other industries.

The impact of kerosene is easily understood. The world needed a better source of light, one that was cleaner, brighter, longer lasting, and more reliable than traditional lighting fuels like wood, whale oil, and paraffin. Kerosene filled the bill and its extraction eventually led to the development of the petrochemical industry on which the world depends so heavily today. For his part, Thomas Willson's pioneering work on calcium carbide and especially acetylene played a valuable role in the development of the automobile and steel industries through the invention of the acetylene torch and the capability to weld heavy metals.

As important as these achievements were, they also highlighted the problems facing Canadian inventors in the nineteenth and early twentieth century, problems that continue to hamper the development of the Canadian economy today. This is the lack of research facilities, markets, and start-up capital.

Many of the country's greatest inventors—including Abraham Gesner, Frederick Gisborne, Thomas Willson, Alexander Graham Bell, Reginald Aubrey Fessenden, W. R. Turnbull, George Desbarats, William Leggo, E. W. Leaver, G. R. Mounce, William Stephenson, and others—were forced to develop their creative abilities and seek funds in other parts of the world because of the lack of these necessities in Canada. This led to dependence on laboratories and research facilities in the United States and Europe, the assignment of patents to companies in other countries, and heavy reliance on European and especially American capital, entrepreneurship, and commercial ability. People and companies in other countries were only too willing to capitalize on the creative ideas of Canadians and exploit them commercially when Canadians were unwilling or unable to do so themselves.

Consider just a couple of examples. Henry Woodward and Mathew Evans, two Canadians who patented the first incandescent light bulb in 1874, were forced to sell their patent to Thomas Edison, who is now generally recognized as the inventor of the electric light bulb. Abraham Gesner was compelled to move to the United States where his patent for kerosene was used to finance the development of the North America Gaslight Company at Hunter's Point, New York. This company eventually became Standard Oil of New Jersey, which today as ExxonMobil remains the largest oil company in the world. Frederick N. Gisborne, chief executive of the Nova Scotia Telegraph Company, had to raise funds in the United States to lay the first transatlantic cable. Thomas L. Willson was forced to sell his acetylene and carbide processes and patents to an American company, and W. R. Turnbull, inventor of the variable pitch propeller, sold his patent to Curtis Wright in the United States.

One of the few Canadian inventors of the nineteenth and early twentieth century who was able to stay in Canada, undertake his research here, and profit from the commercial development of his invention was Ted Rogers, inventor of the batteryless radio. By creating a radio set that plugged into a wall socket rather than using batteries, Rogers gave a boost to the entire broadcasting industry, a boost that helped power the development of the CBC as well as the Rogers communications empire.

Perhaps Alexander Graham Bell and Reginald Aubrey Fessenden best epitomize the problems and predicament of Canadian inventors during this era. Fessenden, who played a key role in research that helped pave the way for the development of radio and later television, did most of his pioneering work at Thomas Edison's Llewellyn Park Laboratory in the United States. He also worked at the United States Company, a subsidiary of the Westinghouse Company, and established a major research facility at Brant Rock in Massachusetts. Alexander Graham Bell also encountered numerous challenges. Like Fessenden, the world-famous inventor of the telephone—who also played a seminal role in the creation of the electric eye, film soundtracks, the metal detector, the hydrofoil boat, the iron lung, and many other devices—was forced to do much of his work in the United States, although he did spend a good deal of time at his summer home and research facility in Baddeck, Cape Breton.

As these examples show, overreliance on foreign and especially American capital, markets, and research facilities has been an impediment to the development and application of Canadian creativity.[*] This fact helps to explain why the country's corporate and political leaders have been so concerned with the need to develop larger markets through free trade agreements, incentives for capital accumulation (especially risk capital), as well as policies to encourage more basic research in Canada. This problem, which lies at the heart of the "integration or independence debate," remains important today and must be dealt with effectively in the future.

However, we are getting ahead of ourselves. Canadian creativity in transportation, communications, agriculture, industry, and resource development continued throughout the twentieth century, as prodigious feats in engineering such as the CN Tower and the Canso Causeway linking New Brunswick and Prince Edward Island and the creation and manufacture of the BlackBerry as well as many other achievements all

---

[*] This theme is developed in detail in J.J. Brown's book *Ideas in Exile*.

confirm. But creativity was starting to manifest itself in other ways as well. As the difficult problems posed by geography were overcome and national wealth increased, new concerns appeared on the Canadian horizon. This creativity manifested itself most profusely in health care, social, legal, and political affairs, education, the arts, sports, recreation, the environment, and, strange as it may seem, humour and comedy.

In health care, for example, Canada's creative achievements can be traced back to the end of the nineteenth century. In 1875 the Hospital for Sick Children was founded in Toronto by a group of women headed by Elizabeth McMaster. Many people believe this was the first hospital in the world devoted entirely to the needs of children. "Sick Kids," the informal name by which the hospital is best known today, is now internationally renowned for its superb facilities and research capabilities. Another Canadian, Sir William Osler, made pioneering contributions to the creation of the world-famous John Hopkins Medical Centre in the United States and became known as "the father of modern medicine" for his innovative approaches to medical training in general and patient care and bedside manner in particular.

Canada's creative contributions to health and medicine were enhanced even further when Frederick G. Banting, Charles H. Best, C. P. Collip, and John Macleod discovered insulin in 1921–22. This accomplishment gained international recognition almost instantly as a result of its promise of saving the lives of people suffering from diabetes. Subsequent pioneers in medicine and health care included Wilder Graves Penfield, an internationally known neurologist and director of the Montreal Neurological Institute; Jean Vanier, who pioneered L'Arche International to assist mentally challenged people throughout the world; June Callwood, who created Casey House and other agencies in Toronto to help people with HIV/AIDS and many other types of illnesses and diseases; and especially T.C. (Tommy) Douglas, who played an instrumental role in establishing the country's universal publicly funded health care system.

Canadians have also made many creative contributions to social, legal, and political affairs. A good example of this occurred at the end of the nineteenth century when the first Women's Institute in Canada was created by Adelaide Hoodless in 1897. This organization grew rapidly to become the Federated Women's Institutes of Canada, the largest women's organization in the world at the time. A number of female trailblazers subsequently left an indelible mark on the country's political and social history. Among the most influential in this regard were Emily Murphy,

Canada's first female judge and the first woman appointed to the bench in the British Empire; Louise McKinney, the first woman to sit in the Alberta legislature in 1917 and the first female elected official in the Empire; Nellie McClung, an outstanding orator and author, who was elected to the Alberta legislature in 1921; and Henrietta Muir Edwards, who was instrumental in creating the forerunner of the YWCA in 1875 and helped to establish the National Council of Women in 1893.

Canadians continued to make many creative social and political contributions in the latter half of the twentieth century. Among the most notable were the drafting of the Universal Declaration of Human Rights in 1947 by John Humphrey from Hampton, New Brunswick, who was director of the Human Rights Division of the United Nations Secretariat and was charged with drafting this remarkable document in conjunction with Eleanor Roosevelt; the peace initiatives undertaken by Lester Pearson during the 1956 Suez Crisis, for which he was awarded the Nobel Peace prize; the passage of the Canadian Bill of Rights in 1960; and the incorporation of this bill into the Canadian Charter of Rights and Freedoms in 1982.

With creative achievements like these to build upon, it is not surprising that many internationally recognized human rights and social activists emerged in Canada during the latter decades of the twentieth century, including Terry Fox, Rick Hansen, Clara Hughes, Maude Barlow, Louise Fréchette, Louise Arbour, Phillipe Kirsch, and many others. In one form or another, these individuals have contributed to the advancement of social justice and legal and political causes here at home and in other parts of the world.

Education is another field where Canadian creativity has been in evidence, particularly during the last century. Among significant developments in this area are the founding in 1899 of Frontier College, one of the world's first colleges devoted to adult education, by Alfred Fitzpatrick, a Presbyterian minister; the pioneering work of Dr. Roby Kidd, who laid the foundation for the development of adult education in Canada and other parts of the world; and the creation of internationally-renowned educational institutions, centres, and institutes, including Pearson College, the Ontario Institute for Studies in Education, the Canadian Institute for Advanced Research, and others.

The arts are yet another area where Canada and Canadians have been highly creative. In the visual arts, this is particularly true of artists who have been primarily concerned with the natural world, such as the Group of Seven, Tom Thomson, Emily Carr, David Milne, Doris McCarthy,

Robert Bateman, and a host of others who have captured the beauty and grandeur of Canada's exquisite landscapes, seascapes, and wildlife. And in recent decades, some of Canada's greatest creative contributions have come in the literary arts. Canadian writers have won many prestigious international awards and surged to the forefront of global recognition and attention. The list of such authors includes Alice Munro, winner of the Nobel Prize in literature, Margaret Atwood, Carol Shields, Margaret Laurence, Mavis Gallant, Rohinton Mistry, Michael Ondaatje, and many others. Building on the literary success of earlier Canadian writers such as Thomas Chandler Haliburton, Susanna Moodie, Catherine Par Traill, Louis Hémon, Lucy Maud Montgomery, Stephen Leacock, Gabrielle Roy, and Anne Hébert, these literary talents have achieved a remarkable amount in bringing Canadian history and culture to the attention of the world.

What is true of the country's writers is also true of its singers and popular musicians. Such well-known figures as Leonard Cohen, Gordon Lightfoot, "Stompin' Tom" Connors, Anne Murray, Bruce Cockburn, the Barenaked Ladies, and Blue Rodeo did a great deal to pave the way for more recent talents such as Céline Dion, Alanis Morissette, Nelly Furtado, Shania Twain, Avril Lavigne, Michael Bublé, Justin Bieber, Drake, and Gordon Downie and the Tragically Hip. Here, too, the country's creative contributions seem out of all proportion to the size of its population. The same is true in classical music and jazz with such talents as Glenn Gould, Angela Hewitt, Marc-André Hamelin, Louis Lortie, Anton Kuerti, Oscar Peterson, Diane Krall, and many others.

Film is still another area where Canadians have exhibited a considerable amount of creativity, both historically and today. Two Canadian brothers, Andrew and George Holland of Ottawa, opened the first movie house in North America in 1894. About the same time, James Freer, a farmer from Manitoba, purchased a combination camera, projector, and printer and became Canada's first filmmaker (and one of the first in the world). He made a number of short films about railroads and life on the Prairies.

In the 1920s, Canada became a pioneer in the development of the documentary film when Robert Flaherty, an American, came to Canada and produced *Nanook of the North*. This was followed, in 1939, by the creation of the National Film Board (NFB) as one of the first and largest public film agencies in the world. Although its founder and first director, John Grierson, a Scot, was a well-established filmmaker before coming to

Canada, he spent much of his professional life here and built the NFB into one of the most highly respected film agencies in the world. According to Grierson, "The National Film Board will be the eyes of Canada. It will, through a national use of cinema, see Canada and see it whole."

Although the NFB was established to inform Canadians about the country's efforts during the Second World War, it went on to make many creative contributions to the art of film, most notably refinement of film documentary and film documentary processes and techniques, the creation of *cinema verité* and multi-screen viewing, and especially in animation as a result of pioneering work in this area by Norman McLaren. Many see McLaren's work as a major influence on some of Walt Disney's animated films, and, much more recently, the innovative techniques in animation, computer graphics, and other areas developed at Sheridan College and elsewhere in Canada to international recognition and acclaim.

While it may come as a surprise, many of Hollywood's best-known actors have been or are Canadians. Many got their start at the CBC, most notably Lorne Greene, Pa in *Bonanza*, William Shatner, Captain Kirk in *Star Trek*, and Christopher Plummer, co-star with Julie Andrews in *The Sound of Music*. Other Canadians who have made it big in Hollywood include Mary Pickford, Marie Dressler, Raymond Massey, Fay Wray, Barry Morse, Chief Dan George, Jay Silverheels, Kate Reid, John Candy, Donald Sutherland, Kiefer Sutherland, Michael J. Fox, Dan Aykroyd, Geneviève Bujold, Mike Myers, Jim Carrey, Ryan Gosling, and many others. As well, many of Hollywood's most outstanding directors, producers, and writers were or are Canadian, including Harry Rasky, Ivan Reitman, Lorne Michaels, Ted Kotcheff, James Cameron, Norman Jewison, and many others. Canadians also made highly original contributions to the development of Hollywood during its early years, especially Sidney Olcett, producer of the first *Ben Hur* movie, Louis B. Mayer, founder of Metro-Goldwyn-Mayer Studios, Jack Warner, founder of Warner Brothers, and Mack Sennett of the Keystone Kops.

Sports are another area where Canadians have made countless creative contributions over the years. Ice hockey is the most obvious example, where Canadian contributions include the first recorded hockey game, played in Montreal on Christmas Day in 1875; the establishment of Stanley Cup competition in 1893; the founding of the National Hockey League in 1917; and numerous victories at the Olympic Games and world championships.

But Canadians have also made important contributions to other sports. Lacrosse was played by an Iroquoian tribe around the Great Lakes who originally called it *Baggataway*, basketball was invented by Dr. James Naismith in 1891, and the first curling club in North America was the Montreal Curling Club, founded in 1807. The first football game was played between McGill University and Harvard University in 1874; the first recorded baseball game took place in Beachville, near Woodstock, Ontario, on June 4, 1838; and the first competition in synchronized swimming took place in Canada in 1923. Canadians also played a prominent role in the development of figure skating and the country has produced numerous Olympic and world champions in this sport, most notably Barbara Ann Scott, Donald Jackson, Kurt Browning, Elvis Stojko, Elizabeth Manley, Jamie Salé, Tessa Virtue, Scott Moir, Meagan Duhamel, Eric Radford, Patrick Chan, and many others.

The environment is yet another field where Canadians have made many creative contributions. Canadian environmentalists and naturalists, including Archibald Blaney (Grey Owl), Ernest Thompson Seton, Jack "Wild Goose" Miner, David Suzuki, Farley Mowat, and Maurice Strong, have helped Canadians understand the priceless value of the natural environment and the need to preserve and protect it. Is it any wonder that one of the world's most aggressive, activist, and inventive environmental organizations—Greenpeace—was created largely by Canadians? With historical and contemporary contributions like these, the country and its citizenry obviously have an important role to play in coming to grips with environmental issues in the future.

It is impossible to conclude this overview without commenting on another area where Canadians have been highly creative. That area is humour and comedy.

There are many historical precedents. In the nineteenth century, one of Canada's best known humorists was Thomas Chandler Haliburton, a judge on the Supreme Court of Nova Scotia. His wit is much in evidence in the characters he created—especially Sam Slick—as well as the satirical books he wrote, most notably *The Clockwork*. A writer active during the first half of the twentieth century, Stephen Leacock, is generally regarded as Canada's greatest humorist. Leacock divided his time between teaching at McGill University and writing satirical books, novels, and short stories. Following closely on Leacock's heels was the CBC radio program *The Happy Gang*. This popular show, broadcast every weekday at lunch time, boosted Canadians' spirits from coast to coast from the early years of the Second World War until the late fifties. Then there were Johnny Wayne and Frank Shuster, popular both here at home and internationally known because of their regular appearances on Ed Sullivan's popular television program in the United States.

Canadian humour and comedy continued to blossom in the latter part of the twentieth century and first part of the twenty-first century. Canadian comedians who have achieved national and international accolades include Mike Myers, Dan Aykroyd, Rich Little, Dave Broadfoot, John Candy, Jim Carrey, Martin Short, Luba Goy, Mary Walsh, and Rick Mercer, among many others. It is a well-known fact that people who laugh together usually stay together and achieve important things.

With this brief glance at Canadian contributions in comedy and humour, our survey of Canadian creativity is complete. It is clear that creativity is Canada's greatest asset. Millions of people in other parts of the world have benefited from it. Given its importance to Canada and the world of the present and the future, it is imperative to invest much more heavily in the development of Canadian creativity. We are talking here not only of the creativity of exceptional Canadians, but the creativity of *all* Canadians from all ethnic backgrounds and socio-economic circumstances in all areas of life. Without this, making the changes in values and behaviour necessary to live in harmony with the natural environment and each other, as well as to play an exemplary role in the world, will not be possible.

CHAPTER FOUR

Diversity Is an Asset

I t is often said that Canadians leave "the best to the last." Surely this statement is true in the sense that many Canadians travel to other parts of the world before they travel a great deal in Canada. Each year, hundreds of thousands of Canadians leave Canada for destinations abroad. Many head to Florida, Arizona, Texas, and California to escape the trials and tribulations of another long Canadian winter, despite often unfavourable currency exchange rates and the high cost of medical insurance. Others travel to Mexico and the Caribbean to "soak up the sun" and enjoy exquisite beaches and crystal-clear waters. Still others travel to Europe to visit museums, art galleries, and world-famous heritage sites, as well as to enjoy good food and drink. And yet others travel to Asia, Africa, South America, or the Middle East to visit family and friends, renew acquaintances with communities and countries once familiar to them, or to experience those parts of the world for the first time.

Let's hope these and other Canadians are able to travel in Canada after their thirst for foreign lands has been quenched, especially as the world's largest travel guide publisher, Lonely Planet, and the *New York Times* both selected Canada as the world's number-one tourist destination—the latter calling it "a world to explore." For what they will discover is a country that is not only extremely beautiful, but also incredibly diverse.

Diversity manifests itself in every domain of Canadian life, from flora, fauna, climate, geography, and the character of the country's natural environment to the many different peoples who inhabit the country and work on its farms and in its offices, factories, and institutions. It would be difficult to find a country in the world more diverse than Canada.

As the second-largest country in the world in geographical size, Canada occupies a land mass of some ten million square kilometres. It stretches across five and a half of the world's twenty-four time zones, from the Atlantic Ocean in the east to the Pacific Ocean in the west and the Arctic Ocean in the north.

The best way to get a good impression of the colossal size and remarkable diversity of the country is to travel by car or train. By rail, it takes almost a week to travel from Saint John's to Victoria. And this is travelling at speeds averaging anywhere from 100 to 150 kilometres an hour!

This seemingly endless expanse of space has always been a source of both inspiration and anxiety for Canadians. On the one hand, there is nothing quite like a colossal land mass with huge areas of wilderness to titillate the imagination, despite the fact that even the boldest acts of abandon often seem like an infinitesimal drop in a bottomless bucket. On the other hand, Canadians are constantly haunted by the fact that the country is so gigantic that it may ultimately prove impossible to govern or keep intact.

A country of this size is bound to have a highly diversified geography. Canada certainly does. There are five distinct regions, each with its own special character.

In the east, there is the Atlantic region, which includes the provinces of Newfoundland and Labrador, Nova Scotia, New Brunswick, and Prince Edward Island, as well as the southeastern portion of Quebec. As the northern extension of New England, with which it shares certain geographical and climatic characteristics, this region is filled with low-lying hills, fertile valleys, and rugged coastlines. There can be no mistaking its maritime quality. Its misty mornings, sea-salt air, historic fishing villages, secluded coves, and pastel-coloured homes can easily be mistaken by even the most experienced traveller for a coastal region in Normandy, the south-west coast of England, the Mediterranean, or, indeed, any coastal region that thrusts its inhabitants outward unto the sea. Perhaps this accounts for the fact that Maritimers have a well-deserved reputation for returning home after spending many years living and working elsewhere. It is hard to be away from this exquisite region for any extended period of time.

Life in this region has always been extremely difficult. Just ask loggers in Newfoundland and Labrador, farmers in Nova Scotia and New Brunswick, or fishermen along the Atlantic coast. These difficulties have been magnified in recent years by the collapse of the Grand Banks fishery as a result of the depletion of fish stocks.

Life in the St. Lawrence lowlands, the second distinct region of Canada, is somewhat easier than in the Atlantic region. Neither, however, yielded to settlers without intense struggle. Accounts of early settlement in southern Ontario and especially Quebec—accounts which have worked their way into the consciousness of Canadians through vivid accounts of homestead life and its challenges by Susanna Moodie, Catherine Parr Traill, Louis Hémon, and others—vary little in detail from accounts of settlement in the Atlantic region. Nevertheless, once permanent settlement was achieved, the St. Lawrence lowlands surrendered their natural bounties with less struggle. As historian Donald Creighton noted in his book *The Commercial Empire of the St. Lawrence*, the natural east-west trading route provided by the river and the Great Lakes furnished the foundation for Canada's continental economic and political expansion. After early hardship and misfortune, many people in this region today enjoy a high standard of living and excellent quality of life.

Summers in this region can get very hot. Often, it is the sultry and humid kind of heat experienced in New Delhi, Singapore, Shanghai, or Hong Kong. Fortunately, this region is the most densely-studded with lakes big and small anywhere in the world. Many of its inhabitants aspire to owning a cottage by a lake where on weekends they can relax, cool off, and recuperate, even if they must travel many hours and endure unbelievable traffic congestion to get there.

This is a region of extremes. In summer, one swelters in the heat. In winter, it is possible to perish in the cold, with temperatures falling well below freezing for extended periods. Springs and falls have a quality—and an aroma—all their own. In spring, the hills and valleys of southern Ontario and Quebec shimmer with thousands of different shades of yellow and green as well as countless wildflowers. In fall, the region is ablaze with colour—the reds, golds, oranges, yellows, and greens of millions of maple, birch, elm, oak, sumac, pine, and spruce trees. The first frost acts as an early warning signal. It turns the leaves magnificent colours. It also warns that another winter is on its way.

The third region of Canada, the interior plains, comprising most of southern Manitoba, Saskatchewan, and eastern Alberta, is also awash with colour. However, here it is the golden glow of wheat, barley, oats, and mustard plants. This is a land of illusions. The land is so flat and the roads so straight at times that one can drive for hours without seeming to get any closer to the towns and cities etched against the clear blue sky. Where else is this true? In Texas, on the pampas of South America, or possibly on the sand dunes of the Sahara?

The fourth distinct region, the Cordillera region, encompasses most of western Alberta and British Columbia and stretches far into the Yukon. Much of this region is mountain country, rivalling in grandeur, the peaks of Switzerland or the Himalayas.

The traveller comes upon Canada's majestic mountain country slowly. Gradually, the prairies give way to the Alberta foothills. Then, suddenly, leaping upward seemingly from nowhere, the Rocky Mountains appear silhouetted against the eternal sky. Largely uninhabited, this range of towering peaks, high plateaus, and alpine meadows cuts British Columbia off from the rest of Canada in many ways. Even though this enormous barrier has been overcome by rail, road, and air travel, it still constitutes a psychic barrier and psychological problem for many Canadians, isolating British Columbians from their counterparts elsewhere in the country. In many ways, British Columbia seems like a different world, further testimony to the geographic diversity of Canada. Warmed by the currents of the Pacific, vegetation along the western and southern parts of this region (including Vancouver Island) has a waxed and profuse quality in summer not unlike a rainforest in tropical Africa, a plantation in the South Seas, or, strange as it many sound, an English country garden.

The country's final region, the Canadian Shield, looms over Canada and Canadians like a colossus. Covering over three million square kilometres in northern Canada, it includes much of the Yukon, Northwest Territories, Nunavut, the Arctic islands, and the northernmost parts of many provinces. While all regions are rich in resources, this is Canada's real "golden horseshoe," forming one of the most abundant storehouses of natural resources in the world. However, it also serves as a vivid reminder of the desolate nature of much of the Canadian landmass. Across approximately 90 percent of the country's area, there is little or no permanent settlement, and in parts of the Canadian Shield, that figure approaches 100 percent. Only the Inuit have mastered the intimate secrets and myriad mysteries of the far north.

Canada's climate, like its topography, is also exceedingly diverse—and variable. No doubt this is why virtually every conversation in Canada starts with remarks about the weather. No matter where people meet—on city streets, in elevators, in parking lots, or at the water cooler—the first comment is almost always about the weather today and what it might be like tomorrow.

While countries nearer the equator have only two seasons—wet and dry—Canada, like other temperate regions, has four: spring, summer, fall, and winter. These seasons shape the country's character, and affect everything from business practices, school schedules, and employment patterns to recreational activities, artistic endeavours, and community celebrations. While most Canadians lament the amount of snow the country receives each winter—indeed, snow is central to Canada's identity, not only for its own citizens but in the eyes of the rest of the world—they also appreciate the variations that take place in the climate from month to month and season to season. While all four seasons have a profound effect on Canada's cultural life, one season, namely winter, is dominant. Here is what journalist and author Bruce Hutchison had to say about this:

> Today it came, the Canadian winter. Snow eddying across the prairies until a woman peering through the windows could not see the neighbour's house and knew she was a prisoner until April. Snow sifting through the streets of Winnipeg and everyone hurrying to get anti-freeze in his radiator, a heater on the windshield, and the vacant lots flooded for the kids' skating rinks. Winter marching eastward over the badlands, placing a puff of snow carefully on every tiny Christmas tree. Winter tiptoeing into an Ontario village by night and all the children awaking with a whoop to get out sleighs and skis and hockey sticks, and the black squirrel in the garden taking one look and disappearing for good.

Not only does winter overpower all the other seasons, but it constantly haunts Canadians, even on the hottest days of summer. There always seems to be a cool day during the summer that reminds Canadians that they are living on borrowed time. As Alden Nowlan, another Canadian author, said in his poem *Shaped by this Land*, "even in August / I can sense the snow clouds."

With a diverse climate come diverse flora and fauna. Many different types of plant life exist throughout the country, such as arctic and alpine tundra, boreal, coniferous, and deciduous forests, western grasslands, and a great deal more. The list of animals inhabiting the country's diverse regions seems similarly endless.

The country's artists perform a valuable service in making Canadians aware of this remarkable diversity. Numerous examples come to mind: Tom Thomson's *Approaching Snowstorm*, *The Jack Pine*, *The West Wind*, and *Autumn Woods*, Frank Carmichael's *Northern Tundra*, J.E.H. MacDonald's *Wild River*, *Buckwheat Field*, *Forest Wilderness*, and *Northern Lights*, Frederick Varley's *Foothills, Alberta*, A.Y. Jackson's

Valley of the Gouffre River, Lawren Harris' *Icebergs*, David Milne's *The Gully*, Emily Carr's *Reforestation*, C.W. Jeffreys' *Western Sunlight*, R. Murray Schafer's *North/White* and *Music for Wilderness Lake*, Harry Somers' *North Country Suite*, Violet Archer's *Northern Landscape*, and the paintings of Glen Loates, Robert Bateman, Freeman Patterson, and other wildlife artists.

The paintings of the Group of Seven play an important role in all this. By making people aware of the remarkable diversity of the Canadian landscape, they broaden and deepen understanding of the highly variegated character of the country's natural environment. In what other country of the world have artists been so active in exposing the richness, diversity, and variety of nature?

When all the many different factors affecting Canada's geography, climate, flora and fauna, and landscape are considered collectively, it is easy to understand why Canadians have an intimate relationship with the natural environment and "the land." It is a relationship that should never be taken for granted, despite the fact that urbanization is causing the country's citizens to lose sight of this relationship.

Indeed, many Canadians feel an ambivalence towards the natural environment. There is the intense love of the natural environment that many Canadians feel. Canada still possesses millions of acres of land virtually untouched by human hands and unseen by human eyes. Where else in the world is this possible today? It is no coincidence that Canadians probably own more outdoor recreational equipment per capita than any other people in the world, taking to pursuits like hiking, canoeing, swimming, skating, skiing, snowmobiling, snowboarding, and tobogganing like ducks to water. Canada also boasts many remarkable national, provincial, and municipal parks as well as numerous conservation areas.

However, there is another, more sinister side to Canadians' relationship with the natural environment—a fear and even contempt that is manifested in the exploitation and abuse of nature, and that historically was engendered by the hardships Canadians are compelled to endure by virtue of the country's challenging geography and climate. As a result, some of Canada's best-known authors, including Margaret Atwood in her book *Survival*, contend that Canadians are victims of a nasty trick perpetrated by nature. This has led to the claim that Canadians have been so terrorized by the harshness of the natural environment that they identify more with the hunted than the hunter. Others, by contrast, argue that Canadians have confronted these obstacles, overcome them, and endured, which gives citizens of the country a kind of heroic quality.

Without doubt, survival is a concern for human beings no matter where they live in the world. Nature seldom surrenders its bounty without struggle. But survival takes on a very different meaning in northern countries like Canada, despite all that has been done in recent years to alleviate this concern. In a country where inhospitable weather can wreak havoc and take lives, survival itself takes on a different meaning. And just as it is impossible for Canadians to escape thoughts of winter on the hottest days of summer, so it is impossible to escape thoughts of survival regardless of how much food is stored in the refrigerator or freezer and how many jackets and overcoats are hanging in the closet. As Margaret Atwood says:

> [T]he main idea is the first one: hanging on, staying alive. Canadians are forever taking the national pulse like doctors at a sickbed: the aim is not to see whether the patient will live well but simply whether he will live at all. Our central idea is one which generates, not the excitement and sense of adventure or danger which The Frontier holds out, not the smugness and/or sense of security, of everything in its place which The Island can offer, but an almost intolerable anxiety. Our stories are likely to be tales not of those who made it but of those who made it back, from the awful experience—the North, the snowstorm, the sinking ship— that killed everyone else.

To be sure, many immigrants to Canada dealt with such fears and worries by settling in areas of the country with geographies and climates similar to their original homes. For instance, Scottish, Irish, Dutch, and German immigrants settled in areas of Nova Scotia, New Brunswick, and southern Ontario that were like those areas of western Europe. This was also true for Ukrainians, Finns, Icelanders, and Scandinavians, who settled in parts of the prairies similar to their onetime homes, and for English people who settled in areas of British Columbia with a climate and topography like that "back home."

Increasingly, however, Canada's population mirrors the remarkable diversity found in nature. Increasing numbers of people from different parts of the world, many with climates and geographies very unlike Canada's, settled here in what has come to be characterized by some as "a land of immigrants."

This diversity was, in fact, present from the very beginning. Though often viewed as a homogenous group, the Indigenous peoples were and still are extremely diverse, with many different tribes, ethnic groups, languages, and dialects. Diversity was also evident among the first European settlers. Historical accounts reveal that there was a German among the Vikings who arrived at L'Anse aux Meadows in Newfoundland in 1001, that many Portuguese were active in the North Atlantic fisheries in the latter part of the fifteenth century, and that a Portuguese colony was even established in Cape Breton from 1520 to 1525. Moreover, although most of the colonists who arrived between 1611 and 1750 hailed from France and Britain, there were also Austrians, Belgians, Croatians, Greeks, Irish, Italians, Dutch, Polish, Scots, Spaniards, Swiss, Jews, Chinese, and Africans among the earliest settlers.

Immigrants from other areas of Europe, the United States, and other parts of the world began to arrive in significant numbers towards the end of the eighteenth century and throughout the nineteenth century. Germans, blacks, and United Empire Loyalists played an important role in this, arriving in significant numbers between 1750 and Confederation. For example, 2,400 settlers from the Palatinate region of Germany arrived in Halifax in 1750. Moreover, blacks settled in Nova Scotia in substantial numbers during and after the period of strong Loyalist immigration, many coming to Canada via the Underground Railroad. Numerous Swiss also arrived at this time, as did many Chinese who came to British Columbia from California and Hong Kong. By the second half of the nineteenth century, Canada's population already had a real multicultural cast.

Nonetheless, Canada was still decidedly British (English, Irish, and Scotch) and French in numbers and character, so much so that the French and British were deemed to be the country's "founding peoples." In fact, it was not until Canada made a strong commitment to immigration in the late nineteenth and early twentieth century that large numbers of immigrants from southern and eastern Europe and elsewhere in the world began to arrive.

Between 1910 and 1915, for instance, more than a million and a half people came to Canada, a number as large or larger than in any other five-year period prior to that time. Among the most prominent groups of immigrants were Ukrainians, Mennonites, Icelanders, Galicians, Dutch, Scandinavians, Russians (Doukhobors), Hungarians, Jews, Poles, Romanians, and Americans. Many of these immigrants manifested a penchant for naming towns and villages after places back home, such as Gimli, Esterhazy, Kaposvar, and so forth.

British Columbia also saw rapid immigration and settlement during this period. Chinese, Sikhs, and East Indians arrived in significant numbers in the late nineteenth and early twentieth centuries, the Chinese playing a crucial role in the construction of railways and especially the CPR, and Sikhs and East Indians contributing to the development of the forestry and lumber industries. Japanese immigrants also began arriving in substantial numbers about this time.

Immigration slowed considerably (and not surprisingly) during the two world wars and the Great Depression. However, it picked up again following both wars, though not on a scale comparable to the period from 1910 to 1915.

Immediately after World War II and continuing into the 1950s and '60s, most immigrants were from war-ravaged European countries. For example, more than 250,000 Italians came to Canada during this period, many settling in Toronto as had some of their earlier counterparts. Large numbers of immigrants from Greece and Portugal also settled in Toronto. As a result, Toronto has some of the largest Italian, Greek, and Portuguese communities outside the borders of those countries. Interestingly, the popular television program *Degrassi High* derived its name from a street in Toronto named after one of the first Italian immigrants to the city, Philip De Grassi.

It was in the years after World War II that the Canadian population started to shed its dominant British and French character and take on a more general European and global character. (Interestingly, it was also during this period that Canada's ties to Britain began to slip away.) According to the 1971 census, for instance, roughly one-quarter of the Canadian population claimed an ethnic origin other than British, French, or Aboriginal. And it was only in 1971 that Canada was officially declared a "multicultural country" by the federal government.

The roots of this declaration can be found in the diverse character of the Canadian population in both the historical and contemporary sense, as well as in other political developments, especially the Quebec Act of 1774. By restoring various aspects of civil law and guaranteeing religious freedom to the French Catholic colonists, the Quebec Act reversed the intention of the Royal Proclamation of 1773 to assimilate the French, the Indigenous peoples, and other ethnic groups into an Anglo-Saxon way of life. In so doing, it recognized the need for equality between the French and British in Canada. Directly and indirectly, this laid the foundation, at least in principle, for interaction between the country's two main ethnic and linguistic groups on the basis of diversity, equality, and integration, rather than uniformity, inequality, and assimilation. This development eventually led to the conviction that *all* of Canada's diverse peoples are equal, regardless of their ethnic origins and cultural differences, a fact that, together with the country's high standard of living, has not been lost on prospective immigrants in recent years.

Accepting and indeed embracing the idea of multiculturalism was, however, far from easy. It took a great deal of tension and conflict over the course of two centuries to bring this about.

Much of this tension and conflict resulted from racist policies and practices. Earlier immigration policies, for example, favoured ethnic groups that Canadians felt could be successfully integrated into the country's culture and existing population, while at the same time discouraging or barring entry to ethnic groups that, it was thought, could not be successfully integrated. These policies were implemented in a variety of ways, such as by drafting lists of "preferred" and "non-preferred" countries, excluding many Asians, Africans, Latin Americans, West Indians, and Jews. There were also campaigns deliberately designed to discourage Chinese and Japanese immigration.

To this must be added the prejudicial treatment and discriminatory practices that many immigrants, refugees, and ethnic groups were subjected to after they arrived in Canada. Examples include the Chinese, East Indian, and Japanese riots in Vancouver in 1907, measures taken against those of Romanian, Czechoslovakian, Hungarian, Polish, Ukrainian, and German descent during the two world wars, and the forcible confinement and internment of more than 22,000 Japanese Canadians as "enemy aliens" during the Second World War.

Many of the problems and grievances that resulted from these policies and practices were aired at the Royal Commission on Bilingualism and Biculturalism, which sat from 1963 to 1965. When the commission concluded that bilingualism and biculturalism were the defining features of Canada, many ethnic groups that were of neither British nor French origin, as well as the country's Indigenous peoples, took exception to this view. While prepared to accept the fact that English and French were the two main languages spoken in Canada, they pointed out that the Canadian population was incredibly diverse and that many groups other than the English and the French had made and continued to make invaluable contributions to the country cultural life that were not adequately recognized in the term "biculturalism."

In 1971, the federal government addressed these concerns by issuing an official response to the Royal Commission's report. That response stated that henceforth Canada would be officially designated a *multicultural* rather than *bicultural* country, paving the way for the present official policy of "multiculturalism within a bilingual framework."

The Trudeau government at that time spelled out the principles, procedures, and funding criteria which would govern this multicultural and bilingual policy:

> The government will support and encourage the various cultures and ethnic groups that give structure and vitality to our society. They will be encouraged to share their cultural expression and values with other Canadians and so contribute to a richer life for us all.
>
> In implementing a policy of multiculturalism within a bilingual framework, the government will provide support in four ways:
>
> First, resources permitting, the government will seek to assist all Canadian cultural groups that have demonstrated a desire and effort to continue to develop a capacity to grow and contribute to Canada, and a clear need for assistance, the small and weak groups no less than the strong and highly organized.
>
> Second, the government will assist members of all cultural groups to overcome cultural barriers to full participation in Canadian society.
>
> Third, the government will promote creative encounters and interchange among all Canadian cultural groups in the interest of national unity.
>
> Fourth, the government will continue to assist immigrants to acquire one of Canada's official languages in order to become full participants in Canadian society.

While there was resistance to the new policy in some quarters, most Canadians endorsed and embraced it as being consistent with the fundamental reality of Canadian cultural life and with the diverse character of the country's population.

The policy spurred the creation of many new institutions at all levels of government and also in the private sector meant to translate policy into practice. The resulting initiatives made it possible for ethnic groups to maintain their cultural identities in the understanding that every ethnic group is entitled to preserve, protect, and develop its culture, customs, and traditions, though not to the exclusion or at the expense of others.

Consistent with the policy of multiculturalism, many types of festivals, fairs, and community celebrations sprang up across the country. One festival that was particularly popular and symbolic of the intent behind Canada's multicultural policy was Caravan. Created in Toronto shortly after the multicultural policy was announced, it epitomized the policy in numerous ways. It provided different ethnic groups with opportunities to share their cultures and customs with others. This highly innovative event was initiated by two Canadians of Ukrainian descent, Leon and Zena Kossar, and took place every fall for many years in what were called "cultural pavilions" located in different parts of Toronto, largely in church basements, community centres, schools, and so forth. Thousands of people flocked to these pavilions by purchasing "passports" that enabled them to enjoy the cuisines, costumes, arts, crafts, and traditions of a cornucopia of cultures. Governments responded positively to this festival because it entailed sharing cultures and cultural experiences rather than isolating them, a prospect that had concerned the federal government a great deal when it made its political commitment to multiculturalism. The last thing Canada needed were cultures and ethnic groups that built walls around themselves and remained separated from each other.

In the years following the announcement of the official policy of multiculturalism, several legislative changes were made that had a direct bearing on the policy's implementation. Most notable were the Citizenship Act of 1977, which abolished the preferential treatment accorded to British subjects who applied for Canadian citizenship; the Canadian Human Rights Act of 1977, which outlawed discrimination on grounds of race, national, or ethnic origin, and colour; and the Charter of Rights and Freedoms of 1982, discussed earlier, which established the equality of all Canadians and their protection under the law regardless of ethnic origin, cultural background, class, gender, colour, and so forth.

Spurred on by the success of multiculturalism, there has been a significant increase in the number of immigrants and refugees coming to Canada over the last several decades, especially those from Asia, the Caribbean, Latin America, the Middle East, and Africa. During these years the country's population truly took on the characteristics of a diverse, cosmopolitan, and multicultural society. Most of those immigrants have settled in major cities, most notably Toronto, Montreal, Vancouver, Winnipeg, Edmonton, Calgary, Halifax, and Ottawa. As a result, the country's population has grown substantially and is much more multilingual, multiracial, and multireligious in character.

As far as size is concerned, Canada's population was roughly thirty-four million at the beginning of the twenty-first century, compared to approximately five and a half million at the beginning of the twentieth century—a more than sixfold increase. Canada's demographic history reveals a remarkable ability to absorb and retain immigrants, despite the fact that early in the twentieth century many immigrants moved to the United States soon after arriving in Canada. Today, the steady inflow of immigration has helped to offset the decline in the birth rate and has kept the country's population growing.

The dramatic change in Canada's ethnic composition has been accompanied by major changes in the population's linguistic and religious character. While English and French remain the most common languages spoken in Canada, many others are now spoken throughout the country on a regular basis. In particular, more recent arrivals from Asia, Africa, Latin America, and the Middle East have dramatically increased the number of Canadians who speak other languages. As the twenty-first century began, more than 5 million people, or one-sixth of the population, indicated their mother tongue was a language other than English or French. Chinese was the third most commonly spoken language, and there were significant numbers of people speaking Punjabi, Arabic, Urdu, Tagalong, Tamil, Dravidian—a family of languages spoken by the traditional inhabitants of parts of India, Sri Lanka, and Pakistan—Pashto, one of the national languages of Afghanistan, Twi, a language spoken by people living in southern Ghana, and Konkani, a language spoken in India.

Just as Canada has become a multicultural and multilingual society, so it has become a multireligious society. While seven out of every ten Canadians were Roman Catholic or Protestant according to the 2001 census, there was a substantial increase in the number of Canadians who reported Islam, Hinduism, Sikhism, and Buddhism as their religion. Those who identified themselves as Muslims recorded the biggest increase, more than doubling from 253,300 in 1991 to 579,600 in 2001. The number of people who identified themselves as Hindu and Sikh increased by 89 percent over this period, while the number of Buddhists increased by 84 percent. Here too immigration was the major factor in this change.

It was impossible for the Canadian population to become increasingly multiracial, multilingual, and multireligious without this affecting many other aspects of cultural life in Canada. This is particularly true of the arts, crafts, cuisine, and so on. There has been an incredible explosion in the variety of artistic practices, hobbies and crafts, restaurants, and even sports and recreational events. This diverse assortment of activities is found not only in the country's largest urban centres but also in numerous smaller towns and cities.

One would expect a country as diverse as Canada in demographic, linguistic, religious, artistic, culinary, geographic, and environmental terms to be diverse in other cultural aspects as well. Canada certainly is. The economy provides an excellent example. While it was once centred on a narrow range of activities and occupations, largely the extraction industries and agriculture, it is now much more diversified. Not only are a vast range of goods and services produced in the primary, secondary, and tertiary sectors of the economy, but Canadians are also employed across the full spectrum of occupations in these sectors, from agriculture, industry, business, and finance to the arts, entertainment, sports, recreation, and tourism.

What is true for the private sector is equally true for the public sector. In education, for instance, the country possesses many different types of educational institutions and programs, policies, and possibilities, primarily because education is a provincial rather than federal matter and consequently every province has its own educational system. There is a similar diversity in politics and government. Because Canada is a federal system, the individual provinces can take their own approaches in many fields, rather than a "one size fits all" solution being imposed by a central government. There are also many different political parties, some national in scope, some limited to one province, as well as departments and agencies at all levels of government, many with their own procedures, policies, practices, and peculiarities. While this complexity produces its fair share of problems, it also produces myriad rewards. For diversity gives rise to new ways of looking at the country and the world, new ways of doing things, new approaches to problems and possibilities, and new attitudes, behaviours, lifestyles, and ways of life.

But it is really in the social realm that diversity manifests itself most conspicuously in Canada. Because of social developments over the last few decades, some of which have occurred throughout much of the world while others are more specific to Canada, the country has become extremely diverse. This is true of sexual preferences, gender possibilities, marital arrangements, family situations, and many other aspects of social life. A new social order has emerged in Canada over the last few decades, one that mirrors the diversity found in the country's cultural life.

Nonetheless, problems of racism, discrimination, and cultural conflict continue to persist, much as they did in earlier periods of history. One significant example of this occurred several decades ago when the Report on Multiculturalism and Racism in Toronto, with the fitting title *Now Is Not Too Late*, was released. (It was referred to as the Pitman Report because the task force that produced it was headed up by Walter Pitman, president of Ryerson Polytechnic Institute.) The impetus for the report was a rash of racially motivated attacks that broke out in Toronto during the winter of 1976–77, largely on the city's transit system. The report was prophetic and visionary in concluding with the following observation and plea: "We live in a great city. But we also live in a 'global village.' It is a world in which more, not less, intermixing of race, skin colour, culture, and religious traditions will take place.... The world of tomorrow will be pluralistic and Metro's citizens will have to develop an affection for diversity."

Similar reports were released in Toronto in the initial years of the twenty-first century, including the Report on Ethno-Racial Inequality in 2000 and the United Way's Report on Poverty by Postal Code in 2004. They affirmed the Pitman Report's findings, and concluded that there is a strong interconnection (or "intersection," to use a term now popular with sociologists) among poverty, immigration, racism, and visible minorities. In order to prevent "pockets of poverty" in Canada's largest city from becoming larger, the authors of the United Way report recommended greater investment in affordable housing, increases in the minimum wage and social assistance, improvements in social infrastructure, and the building of strong neighbourhoods and multicultural services to help immigrants integrate more fully into Canadian society.

Other factors have also necessitated the need for intensified government measures to ensure security, stability, and the successful integration into the Canadian population. For one thing, in today's globalized society there is much more interaction among different ethnic and racial groups, both in Canada and around the world. This is a positive development in many ways, but also poses challenges in terms of public safety. Secondly, as Robert Putnam pointed out in his popular book *Bowling Alone*, in today's society increasing numbers of people are withdrawing from community life and from involvement in service clubs and religious organizations. Given this, levels of trust, cooperation, and collaboration in the population generally must be significantly increased, and even more so in countries that are ethnically diverse. It is therefore important to put a great deal of stress on *shared* experiences if the shortcomings of multiculturalism are to be addressed successfully and people with vastly different ethnic, racial, religious, social, and linguistic backgrounds and origins are to live in peace and harmony rather than conflict and confrontation.

This problem has been hotly debated in many parts of the world in recent years, particularly in Europe because of the large influx of immigrants and refugees into European countries and particularly as a result of the Syrian crisis. Many European countries have abandoned the idea of multiculturalism in favour of the idea of *interculturalism*, which is predicated on the belief that much more interaction and exchange needs to take place between different cultures, peoples, and ethnic groups. The fear is that multiculturalism can result in ethnic groups turning inward rather than outward, getting so caught up in their own cultures, traditions, and religions that they ignore or downplay those of others.

Despite such developments in Europe and also in the United States as a result of the 2016 presidential election, Canadians have maintained their commitment to the country's official policy of multiculturalism and have done so for a very good reason. *It has worked well on the whole since it is first introduced, and is still working well today.* This is because, unlike many European countries and the United States, Canada's official policy of multiculturalism within a bilingual framework has allowed immigrants and refugees from other parts of the world to maintain their cultures, identities, and traditions while simultaneously enabling them to participate in the development of Canada and Canadian culture in many different ways.

The benefits that have accrued to Canada from this policy are enormous. In the first place, it has substantially expanded the realm of choice for most Canadians, something which is evident in virtually every dimension of the country's cultural life. This has resulted in the creation of many different jobs and career possibilities, diverse educational programs, countless more artistic, culinary, athletic, and recreational activities, and broader access to different values, perceptions, lifestyles, and ways of life.

Multiculturalism, pluralism, and diversity have also made it possible for Canadians to learn a great deal more about the world around them by capitalizing on the insights, beliefs, and customs of all the diverse peoples and ethnic groups that comprise the Canadian population. As members of the Bilingual and Bicultural Commission were compelled to recognize, the country has reaped enormous advantages from such diversity.

It is impossible to attend an artistic event, see the names of graduates from the country's high schools, community colleges, and universities, or read about the creative achievements of Canadians without realizing how much the country's many different ethnic groups have contributed to Canadian culture and the country's overall way of life. Whether it be through the Olympic or Pan Am Games, world championships, spelling bees, festivals, community celebrations, international conferences, or countless other events, Canadians are aware of how much can be accomplished by drawing on the talents of all the country's different ethnic groups.

It is especially important to recognize and capitalize on this asset because at present diversity in the human and natural realms is being threatened in all parts of the world. As forests are chopped down, animals hunted down, ecological habitats decimated and destroyed, species lost, customs and languages disappear, and ways of life and entire cultures vanish or collapse, diversity is clearly under siege. The need to protect and preserve diversity has become one of the most pressing issues facing humanity.

That is why Canada was one of the initiators and principal formulators—as well as one of the strongest advocates—of UNESCO's Universal Declaration of the Diversity of Cultural Expressions, signed in 2005. This declaration was passed in order to protect diversity in every society despite strong pressures to stamp out differences and promote similarities and uniformity. Not only was Canada actively involved in the original creation of this declaration, but it was also the first signatory and has been at the cutting edge of international efforts to promote and implement it ever since. For similar reasons, the International Coalition for Cultural Diversity has its headquarters in Canada. This organization is deeply committed to developing the multilateral framework of principles, rules, regulations, and practices required to protect and enhance diversity throughout the world.

Nevertheless, diversity has its risks as well as its benefits. This has become steadily more apparent in recent years with escalating conflict among different races and religious and ethnic groups. While there are no easy answers to such problems, there is without doubt an urgent need for more interaction and dialogue between such groups in Canada and elsewhere. There is an equal need to develop a strong, united, and shared culture in Canada—a culture that is based on enjoying certain commonalities while simultaneously respecting, protecting, and appreciating certain differences.

The key to this lies in coming to grips with the fact that Canadian culture is far more than the sum of all the many different cultures and peoples that contribute to it. More fundamentally and essentially, it is the common set of values, beliefs, customs, and traditions that all Canadians share despite their ethnic, racial, religious, demographic, and geographical differences. Included in this common set of values are dedication to a land of great beauty, size, and grandeur; recognition of the valuable contributions made by previous generations of Canadians to the development of Canada and Canadian culture; devotion to equality, freedom, and democracy regardless of race, religion, age, gender, ability, or disability; devotion to universal health care and social welfare; recognition of the rights, freedoms, traditions, and customs of others; willingness to consult, compromise, and make concessions; adherence to peace, order, and security; and commitment to national unity and Canadian identity. These "commonalities of experience," as many of them were termed at the Citizen's Forum on Canada's Future in 1990, are deeply imbedded in the country's culture, history, and overall way of life. They need to be constantly asserted and reasserted if the risks and dangers inherent in diversity, multiculturalism, and pluralism are to be addressed successfully in the future.

This is why endeavouring to achieve and maintain "unity in diversity" in all segments of Canadian society and all sectors of the country's cultural life is so essential. Doing so focuses attention on the creation of a comprehensive Canadian culture that all Canadians can participate in, enjoy, contribute to, benefit from, and respect. Canada, perhaps more than any other country in the world, is a microcosm of the global macrocosm in demographic, environmental, and cultural terms. If Canada and Canadians can deal effectively with diversity, if they can achieve and maintain unity in diversity, this accomplishment will auger well not only for Canada itself in the remaining decades of the twenty-first century but also for the rest of the world.

CHAPTER FIVE

Assessing the Present Situation

T he beginning of the twenty-first century was greeted by Canadians and, indeed, people all around the world with a great deal of enthusiasm and optimism. Not only was it the beginning of a new century, but also the beginning of a new millennium. It was time for a momentous celebration.

No expense was spared. Countless events were planned and conducted, and festivities of every conceivable type were held in Canada and elsewhere as people realized this was a "once in a lifetime opportunity" that would not occur again for a thousand years. Incredible displays of fireworks were set off on that memorable night that made displays on more routine festive occasions seem insignificant by comparison.

Unfortunately, the optimism and enthusiasm did not last long. The terrorist attacks of September 11, 2001 shocked the entire world. People could not believe what they were seeing on their television sets or hearing about on their radios as the upper echelons of the Twin Towers of the World Trade Center in New York were engulfed in flame and eventually came crashing down. Buildings viewed by many as symbols of world power, influence, and dominance lay crumpled in gigantic piles of rubble. It was difficult to believe that an attack of this magnitude against the most powerful nation on earth could have been planned and carried out.

The immediate concern was for the victims of the catastrophe, whether the passengers aboard the doomed airliners, workers at the World Trade Center and the Pentagon, and the first responders who had risked their lives to try to rescue those trapped in the burning buildings. Their heroics, including those of myriads of firefighters and police officers whose job was to try to help regardless of personal costs and consequences, were exemplary in every respect. Numerous tales of heroic deeds and extraordinary acts of bravery and courage were soon being told about that never-to-be-forgotten day.

It was not long after these deplorable attacks that people started to ask who was responsible for them. Who planned these attacks? Where were they planned? And most importantly, why were they executed? The immediate answer was that the attacks were conducted by a group of terrorists who had been planning them for months and possibly years, and who were hostile to the United States, Americans, and the American way of life. But how were they able to pull off these attacks and how did they gain access to United States and to the planes and weapons necessary to execute the attacks?

As time wore on, two things became apparent. The first was that terrorism had to be confronted head on and overcome in all countries of the world and not just the United States through more effective safety and security measures. Clearly much more time, effort, and money would have to go into ensuring that citizens are safe, borders secure, and surveillance and information systems in place to root out terrorists wherever they are living in the world and planning their evil deeds.

The second was that there were significant numbers of people in the world, and possibly even entire countries, who were hostile to the United States because they didn't like the direction the United States was taking the world and the influence it exerted. Much of this hostility was directed at the way of life that was sanctioned in the United States and other Western countries, especially with respect to materialistic, exploitative, and oppressive economic, commercial, corporate, and political practices and rapidly escalating inequalities in income and wealth, as well as Western values concerning the separation of church and state. The United States, the Twin Towers, and the Pentagon were seen as the epitome of everything that was wrong in the world and the attacks were required to set things right in the minds of the people who harboured these feelings and committed these despicable deeds.

The United States reacted to the attacks swiftly and forcefully. The focus was on "homeland security" and "rooting out terrorists" as measures were introduced at every level to tighten up security procedures and ferret out terrorists whether they were living in the United States or elsewhere in the world. Special emphasis was placed on al-Qaeda, the Taliban, and especially Osama bin Laden, as they had been the most visible, vocal, and active in the attacks. However, concern was also expressed over the need to stamp out terrorism in other countries.

Located next door to the United States, Canada was instantly affected by the 9/11 attacks. Almost immediately, governments across the country sprang into action and instituted similar measures in Canada that were designed to ensure that Canadian citizens were safe and that the infrastructure was in place to prevent terrorist attacks in this country. Safety and security became "trigger words" and "key issues" as municipal, provincial, and territorial governments, and especially the federal government, endeavoured to ensure that terrorists were identified and dealt with swiftly and severely. While Canada had been at peace for decades, it suddenly found itself in a position where peace could no longer be taken for granted. Similar attacks could occur at any time in Canada and not just in the United States, especially given the close proximity and intimate relationship between the two countries.

Particular attention was paid to the "longest undefended border in the world," especially when some claims were made that the terrorists who committed these atrocious acts had gained access to the United States through Canada. As a result of these and other concerns, Canadians travelling to the United States found wait times at airports and borders much longer. Every suitcase, trunk, and handbag had to be opened and every item meticulously checked. Soon, Canadians were required to hold passports to enter the United States after decades and indeed centuries of virtually free and unrestricted movement between the two countries.

It was evident that a "new order" was beginning to take shape in the world. While terrorist attacks were nothing new, most had been confined to individuals, institutions, and small groups. The 9/11 attacks were very different. They were seen and interpreted as attacks on an entire nation, intended to bring the United States to its knees and calculated to make Americans feel pain and feel it at home, thereby making a clear statement to the entire world.

As horrific as the attacks were, they were also a signal that the world was changing, and changing very rapidly and dramatically. The world was becoming "all of a piece" in a way it never had been before. Whereas the focus for centuries had been on tribes, towns, cities, regions, countries, and more recently "nation-states"—and, in the case of the United States, Great Britain, and a handful of other European countries, "empires"—the focus was now shifting to "*the world as a whole*" and with it the "*world system.*" Issues affecting the entire world were thrust into the forefront, starting to drive the agenda. That trend is expected to continue much more fully in the future.

The origins of this seismic shift in the world situation can be traced back to developments after the Second World War. This is when truly *world* organizations such as the United Nations, the International Monetary Fund (IMF), the World Bank, and the General Agreement on Trade and Tariffs (GATT) were created. They were designed to look at problems and issues from an international or global perspective rather than from local, regional, or national perspectives. They were also expected to make decisions based on what was in the best interests of the world as a whole and not just those of specific countries and regions, although it was clear that the Western world in general and the United States in particular would continue to exercise an incredible amount of power, influence, and control over the affairs of the aforementioned organizations.

This shift in the way the world is perceived and interpreted has been strengthened considerably over the last few decades through the creation of many more world organizations, the transformation of the General Agreement on Trade and Tariffs into the World Trade Organization (WTO), the expansion of the United Nations and its many departments and agencies, and a great deal else. The emphasis in these cases, and others, has been, and still is, on the creation of institutions that are much more comprehensive in an international sense in their dealings, operations, policies, and practices.

The word that is usually used to describe this phenomenon is *globalization*. It has come to mean the remarkable amount of interaction going on among the diverse peoples, institutions, countries, economies, cultures, and civilizations of the world. While globalization has been occurring for centuries, it has become far more pronounced over the last two decades. It has also acquired two specific but very different meanings. The first is all the interconnections and interactions that are going on between the diverse countries and peoples of the world. The second is the projection of Western values, beliefs, practices, and ways of life onto people and countries in other parts of the world.

The International Monetary Fund has identified four main reasons for globalization: growth in international trade; increased capital movements and investments; stepped-up, large-scale migrations of people; and, especially, the improvement in global communications and dissemination of information and ideas throughout the world.

For centuries, the world was divided into thousands of small groups, units, and regions. Now, globalization is rapidly producing "one world." This is making it possible to end the use of many divisive, derogatory, and demeaning terms—terms such as First World or Third World, as well as terms such as "developed" and "developing" countries—and talk instead about "the world as a whole," of which all people and countries are now integral parts. This has been accompanied by a sense that people are becoming "global citizens" and not just citizens of particular countries.

One of the main advantages of globalization is that it has made it possible for many countries in Asia, Africa, Latin America, and the Caribbean to experience more rapid rates of economic growth, improve their standards of living, and enjoy a better quality of life. This has been realized through the opening up of economic and political systems in these countries, increased trade and investment, improved educational systems, and the use of new technologies.

China and India are often held up as examples of countries that are benefiting immensely from globalization. After centuries of relative isolation, these countries have grown rapidly in economic terms in recent years because they have embraced globalization and capitalized on its numerous benefits. This has enabled them to increase their people's standard of living, sell more products and services at home and abroad, and stimulate more consumption and investment activity. And what is true for these countries is also true for many others.

While globalization has brought the world closer together, it has also exposed the incredible diversity and complexity that exists in the world, and the many differences among peoples, countries, cultures, civilizations, religions, and ways of life. It has also exposed many problems, pressures, tensions, and conflicts. There are two sides to globalization. Not only does globalization have many strengths and rewards, but it also has some fundamental drawbacks and shortcomings. And something else is true, too. While many countries have benefited from globalization, others have not been so fortunate since it has placed limitations, demands, and expectations on them that have been difficult if not impossible to meet. This problem will have to be addressed fully and effectively in the future if the world is to become a more harmonious and secure place, rather than more chaotic and dangerous.

Included among the many drawbacks of globalization are the huge disparities in income and wealth that exist throughout the world, the ownership and control of the bulk of the world's wealth by a tiny fraction of extremely rich people, institutions, and countries, and the concentration of power and influence in the hands of a small coterie of elite groups and multinational corporations that are more concerned with the bottom line than with human welfare and environmental well-being.

To this must be added the fact that a significant backlash against globalization has begun to occur in recent years. This is most acute in countries that have suffered from lower rates of economic growth, the out-sourcing of jobs to other countries, and the movement of industry to other parts of the world in order to capitalize on lower labour costs. This back-lash has been most conspicuous in a number of European countries such as Greece, Spain, and Italy, as well as in other parts of the world that have experienced slower rates of economic growth, increased unemployment, the loss of manufacturing jobs, and, in some cases, escalating debts, deficits, and the introduction of various types of austerity measures. The problems of southern Europe have been aggravated by the turmoil in the Middle East and the exodus of large numbers of refugees from that region as well as North Africa into Europe in the search for a better life.

Globalization has also been accompanied by the disappearance of many traditional identities, customs, languages, heritages, and cultures, by resentment in certain parts of the world of the highly materialistic way of life and ruthless commercial practices that appear to be an inevitable consequence of globalization, and many other factors.

The downside of globalization and its numerous shortcomings have produced a great deal of anxiety and hostility, as many people have decided it is time to strike back and prevent globalization from ruining their countries and their lives. There are many examples of this. It is manifested most conspicuously in the resistance of many European coun-tries to opening up their borders to even more immigrants and refugees and also in the decision by Britain to leave the European Union. It mani-fested itself even more poignantly in the election of Donald Trump as president of the United States in 2016. Much of Trump's winning agenda was based on "making America great again" by showing more concern for working-class people and their economic situation, pulling out of the Trans Pacific Partnership (TPP), renegotiating the North American Free Trade Agreement (NAFTA), reducing outsourcing and preventing the movement of American companies to other parts of the world, and by tightening up borders and immigration policies, especially in relation to immigrants from the Middle East as well as Mexico. These developments, and others that might be cited, indicate that the world of the future could be shaped much more significantly by anti-globalization movements, protectionism, and restrictions on the movement of labour, capital, and companies.

Like all countries, Canada is being affected by these two different dimensions of globalization in a whole series of deep, diverse, and dynamic ways. On the positive side of the ledger, there is no doubt that the country and its citizenry have profited greatly from the benefits, opportunities, and advantages that accrue from globalization, particularly expanded economic, political, educational, technological, artistic, and scientific opportunities, including interactions with countries in Asia, Africa, Latin America, and the Caribbean where Canada has had few such relationships in the past.

Globalization in this positive sense goes even deeper and farther for Canada and Canadians. In fact, it is one of the most essential requirements for achieving the breakthrough required for the country and its citizenry in the remaining decades of the twenty-fist century to realize their full potential and play an exemplary role in the world.

There is a straightforward reason for this. Since Canada was very dependent on France and Britain in earlier periods of history, and the United States more recently, the country's international sector is underdeveloped in size and stature compared to most other industrialized countries. As a result, globalization provides a unique opportunity for Canadians to make a "quantum leap" in international relations and foreign policy. For, perhaps more than any other country, Canada has an incredible amount to contribute to the world of the future, especially in terms of its creativity, diversity, pluralism, inclusiveness, and ability to deal with complexity and achieve "unity in diversity." For these and other reasons to be discussed later, the country and its citizenry should embrace globalization and take full advantage of its benefits in the future.

Nevertheless, it is necessary to emphasize that globalization also has risks and dangers for Canada and not only benefits. One is falling into "the staples trap" that Harold Innis and other Canadian economists warned against. It would be a mistake of major proportions for the country and its citizenry to get so caught up in natural resource development and the exportation of natural resources to other parts of the world that they lose sight of how important it is to persevere with the quest to develop a comprehensive, integrated, and more diversified economy.

This will not be possible without aggressive action to achieve it, especially as things seem to be moving in the opposite direction at present due to Canada's munificent supply of natural resources. Indeed, Canada could easily find that it has become a resource basket not only for the United States but also for other countries.

But there is another potential danger here. Globalization has led to corporations being given many special privileges, as well as being accorded a very powerful role in the world. Such developments could result in reductions in the size, importance, and power of governments, the deregulation of many more markets, and the signing of more trade agreements designed to advance the interests of corporations and wealthy elites. This matter will have to be addressed fully and effectively in the future if the necessary checks and balances are to be established and maintained between the public sector and the private sector.

Until very recently, Canada was a staunch supporter and strong advocate of this particular type of globalization. During this time, significant cuts were made in Canada with respect to funding of numerous not-for-profit, ethnic, and charitable organizations, as well as the budgets of the Canadian Broadcasting Corporation, the Canadian International Development Agency, and many other institutions and agencies. Moreover, a "trade" rather than "aid" approach was taken to Canada's international relations, a great deal of scientific and empirical research was curtailed or cut back, and a more commercial approach was taken to immigration, international affairs, and foreign policy. This was accompanied by efforts to downsize the public sector as well as to "balance the books" and reign in government debts, deficits, and spending whenever they ran counter to the principles of globalization, conservatism, and free trade.

Despite this, it is on the environmental front that conflicting views and opinions over this particular form of globalization were and are still most in evidence. Throughout the world, major conflicts have erupted between individuals and institutions that support this type of globalization and individuals and institutions that support environmental protection, preservation, and conservation. While evidence was mounting daily that climate change and global warming were realities and human actions were largely responsible for them, proponents of the aforementioned ideologies, policies, and practices contended that these problems did not exist at all or were grossly exaggerated. When 97% of the world's scientists claimed that human influences on climate change were clear and undeniable and that global warming was having a detrimental effect on human and natural systems, as documented in detail by the Intergovernmental Panel on Climate Change in 2014, many conservative governments refused to accept this conclusion and sought out the few remaining scientists who disagreed with the findings of the panel.

This is where matters stand at present on this issue, except that more and more people and countries are experiencing the effects of climate change firsthand, not only in Asia, Africa, Latin America, and the Caribbean, but also in Europe, Canada, and the United States where hurricanes, droughts, forest fires, heat waves, tornadoes, and coastal flooding are becoming more commonplace as well as more conspicuous and severe. This development has caused a major shift in the discussions with respect to climate change: it is no longer a case of whether or not climate change and global warming exist, but, rather, how serious they are, and, much more importantly, what must be done about them. The issue was further highlighted when Pope Francis issued a papal encyclical on the matter that was widely publicized in the United States and other parts of the world.

How this matter will be dealt with in the future has been fundamentally altered by the election of Donald Trump and the fact that after the 2016 elections, the Republican party controlled the White House, the Senate, and the House of Representatives. The U.S. Supreme Court is also controlled by a conservative majority. There are indications that there could be a return to earlier denials with respect to climate change and the environmental crisis, especially when in 2017 Trump pulled the U.S. out of the Paris climate accord, much to the consternation of many environmental organizations, activists, and movements throughout the world.

And this brings us to the environmental situation in Canada. Like globalization, the environment is a hotly debated topic in Canada, with people coming down on both sides of the issue. While some Canadians believe too much is being made of environmental concerns which, they say, do not pose the serious threat that many environmentalists contend, others believe that it is a life-and-death matter that must be dealt with without delay.

What was particularly disturbing for many Canadians was the way the environmental situation was handled by the Conservative government led by Prime Minister Stephen Harper. Not only did this government withdraw from the Kyoto Protocol in 2011—despite the fact that Canada had been actively engaged in the original negotiations to create the protocol as far back as 1997—but the government dragged its feet on virtually all major environmental issues during its time in power. This lack of action severely damaged Canada's reputation and image in the world and helps to explain (along with other factors) the election of Justin Trudeau's Liberals in 2015.

The solution embraced by many political, governmental, and environmental leaders in Canada and around the world is the immediate reduction of carbon emissions as agreed at the Summit on the Environment in Paris in 2015 and, far more importantly, the need to shift in the world from "unsustainable" to "sustainable" development. Sustainable development is designed to take the natural environment and the needs and interests of future generations fully and forcefully into account.

Like globalization, the origins of the concept of sustainable development can be traced back several decades and specifically to the creation of the United Nations Environmental Programme in 1972, the establishment of the United Nations World Commission on Environment and Development—the Bruntland Commission—between 1983 and 1987, the United Nations Conference on Environment and Development in Rio de Janeiro in 1992, and many other initiatives and activities.

Interestingly, two Canadians played a seminal role in these developments in general and the evolution of the idea of sustainable development in particular. The first was Maurice Strong, a highly controversial and provocative Canadian who walked the fine line between the private sector and corporate development on the one hand and the public sector and political development on the other. As the first director of the United Nations Development Programme, as well as the driving force behind the creation of the Bruntland Commission and the 1992 Rio de Janeiro conference, Strong has often been described as "the father of the modern environmental movement," despite the fact that he had numerous corporate dealings, holdings, connections, and interests over the years. The other Canadian was James MacNeill, who served as the director responsible for environmental issues at the Organization for Economic Cooperation and Development (OCED) in Paris for several years, Secretary General of the World Commission on Environment and Development, and who was principal author of the commission's report, entitled *Our Common Future*, that promoted the idea of sustainable development.

Since that time, most institutional and governmental leaders in the world have bought into the idea of sustainable development and endorsed it fully. This fact has affected the entire way development is perceived, defined, and practiced, resulting in pressure to ensure that precautions are taken to protect the natural environment and the needs and interests of future generations whenever environmental and developmental matters are considered and addressed.

It wasn't long after the introduction of the idea of sustainable development that the United Nations created a set of Millennium Development Goals (MDG's). These goals were initially put forward in 2000, at the very beginning of the new century and new millennium. Included were commitments to greater income equality, overcoming poverty, improving access to water, reducing child mortality, and increasing primary school enrolments. While significant progress was made in realizing some of these goals—especially raising millions of people out of abject poverty, increasing global primary school enrolment, and increasing access to clean drinking water—other goals were not met and it was concluded overall that the goals that had been set were too ambitious and unrealistic.

Nevertheless, this did not deter the United Nations from creating a new set of *Sustainable* Development Goals (SDG's) (emphasis mine) at the United Nations Conference on Sustainable Development in Rio de Janeiro in 2012. These goals were designed to strike a more effective balance between what were viewed by the United Nations at that time as the three basic factors underpinning sustainable development: economic, social, and environmental.

In 2015, a whole new set of goals was announced by the United Nations. Called the 2030 Agenda, it established seventeen sustainable development goals for the fifteen-year period between 2015 and 2030, including ending poverty and hunger, achieving gender equality, reducing income inequality, and so on. With a staggering estimated price tag of $ 3.3 trillion to $ 4.5 trillion per year, these goals came at a time when many countries were struggling with various economic and fiscal problems. Nevertheless, the UN claimed that the 2030 Agenda was imperative because it is concerned with "healing the planet" and focuses attention on the "five key P's"—people, planet, prosperity, peace, and partnership. In a speech at the opening ceremony of the UN's Sustainable Development Summit in Istanbul in 2015, Ban Ki-moon, then Secretary General of the UN, called on the world to adopt and embrace the 2030 Agenda and its goals, regardless of the difficulties involved in doing so.

While the environmental crisis in general and climate change in particular have become one of the most urgent problems facing humanity, huge and growing disparities in income and wealth are not far behind. Concern over this problem has escalated rapidly in recent years, especially when it became apparent that a tiny portion of incredibly rich and powerful people own or control the bulk of the world's wealth.

This issue came to a head with the "Occupy Wall Street" movement and the protests in Zucotti Park in New York's Wall Street financial district in 2011. Chanting "We are the 99%," thousands of protestors met in the park to condemn the blatant inequalities in the distribution of income and wealth as well as the hollowing out of the middle class, political corruption, excessive corporate influence on government and the political process, high levels of unemployment among young people and blue-collar workers in many if not all parts of the world, extravagant payouts to corporate executives, and the austerity measures many governments were forced to impose that necessitated severe cutbacks in spending on necessary programs and services.

With this movement has come another type of backlash in recent years. It is not yet another backlash against globalization, although it is connected with that backlash in many ways, but, rather, a backlash against "the establishment." While this backlash was manifested in the Occupy Wall Street movement and related protests, it has focused more fundamentally on the nexus between wealthy and powerful elites, multinational corporations, political parties, and the like. The goal, as viewed by increasing numbers of people, is to reward the rich and penalize everyone else, to sustain the power, control, and influence the establishment has over the world system, and, in short, to maintain the political and economic status quo. This has resulted in many right-wing populist movements, such as those evident in France, Italy, Scandinavia, Holland, Eastern Europe, and especially the United States.

One of the earliest signs of this backlash and the movement that accompanies it was the election of Rob Ford as mayor of Toronto in 2010. His campaign and election were predicated largely on "ending the gravy train" that corporations, developers, and political parties enjoyed and, with this, restoring "power to the people." The trend was much more in evidence during the American elections of 2016, first in the "revolution" advocated by Bernie Sanders to restore power to labourers and the working class, then by attacks on Hillary Clinton and the Democrats as the very epitome of the establishment and establishment politics, and finally in the election of Donald Trump, who (despite being a billionaire himself) claimed to be the champion of "the people and all Americans," not just the rich, the powerful, and the privileged.

In recent years, inequalities in income and wealth, the hollowing out of the middle class, and especially the failure of trickle-down economics to improve the lot of the less-favoured socio-economic classes have made "poverty" a growing concern worldwide as well as in Canada. For a country like Canada with a high standard of living and excellent quality of life, it is unconscionable that there remain so many poor people and especially children living in poverty. This makes the elimination of poverty—not only internationally through UN's Sustainable Development Goals and 2030 Agenda but also in Canada through specifically designed policies and practices—a high priority.

This is equally true of a number of other major demographic issues confronting Canada and the world. One of the most important is the aging population. According to 2015 statistics provided by the World Health Organization, the proportion of the world's population over 60 will almost double from 12 percent to 22 percent between 2015 and 2050. While this is a cause for celebration in certain ways—people are living longer than they once did—it is also a cause for concern because the costs of looking after the elderly are already very high and threatening to escalate out of control in Canada and other countries.

It boggles the mind to imagine where the money will be found to care for the elderly in future years, especially given escalating health care costs. Moreover, a whole new range of debilitating diseases are manifesting themselves with increased frequency, largely because people often live into their seventies, eighties, and even nineties. As a result, diseases like multiple sclerosis, ALS, Parkinson's, and many forms of dementia (such as Alzheimer's) are affecting growing numbers of people and proving extremely difficult to contend with, both for those suffering from these diseases themselves as well as their families and caregivers.

Although Canada is in a much better position to deal with these problems than most countries, and while longevity brings with it many benefits, the fact that 31% of the Canadian population will be 60 or older by 2050 (according to the GlobeAgeWatchIndex of 2013) means that Canadians and the country's governments, hospitals, and health care agencies and providers will have to brace themselves for a very demanding and exceedingly difficult situation.

Another important demographic change involves the changing role of women and their fight for equality. While some important strides have already been made, an enormous amount remains to be accomplished. Recent studies show that Canada has dropped from first place to thirty-fifth in the World Economic Forum's annual ranking of gender equality. Women in Canada earn about $ 8,000 less per year than men when doing work of equal value, according to the Canadian branch of Catalyst; the Canadian gender gap in pay is twice the global average, according to the United Nations; nearly half of the companies listed on the Toronto Stock Exchange do not have a single woman on their boards of directors; Canadian women account for only about 8 percent of senior corporate managers; and women are over-represented in the lowest-paying, most precarious jobs, which are largely in the service sector. To be sure, women have made strong strides in fields such as medicine, law, and business administration, but much remains to be done.

Such problems are not limited to Canada, of course. In many parts of the world, the lack of educational opportunities for girls is a particular challenge. As Malala Yousafzai, the Pakistani girl shot by Taliban soldiers in 2012 for advocating education for girls, has declared, educating girls is every bit as important as educating boys. As a prominent human rights advocate and recent recipient of the Nobel peace prize, she had the courage to declare that girls deserve the same treatment as boys, nothing more *but emphatically nothing less.* In so doing, she touched people in all parts of the world, including Canada, where she spoke to Parliament and was made an honorary Canadian citizen, with her commitment, dedication, and bravery.

Much will need to be done to ensure that gender equality is achieved in all areas of both Canada's and the world's cultural life, including pay equity in all jobs and professions, equal representation in business, government, politics, and education, and so forth. The Liberal government's effort to achieve gender equality in the cabinet and make it as diverse and representative as possible marks a significant step in the right direction. Not only is it consistent with the new demographic reality, but it has been well received in Canada and elsewhere, and as such provides a concrete illustration of Canada's ability to play an exemplary role in the world of the future.

Another important priority involves Canada's Indigenous peoples. Not only is it necessary to make amends for their deplorable treatment in the past; it is also vital in the future to ensure the preservation of their cultures, identities, languages, traditions, and ways of life; improve their standards of living, quality of life, socio-economic status, and well-being; honour their land claims and treaty agreements; advance their educational prospects; and respect them as full contributors to all aspects of Canadian culture.

The same holds true, though in a different sense, for the country's young people. Much more consideration will have to be given to early childhood education, changes in elementary, secondary, and post-secondary education, and especially employment opportunities, prospects, and practices once young people leave school. It is unacceptable that so many Canadians in their teenage years and twenties are compelled to carry huge debts after finishing their post-secondary education and are unable to find meaningful work or, sometimes, any work at all. Young people deserve to have meaningful, constructive, and fulfilling work in their areas of training and interest where they can develop their creativity and potential to the greatest extent.

Yet another demographic trend bound to have a profound impact on Canada and the world is population growth. While the world as a whole faces severe challenges in terms of sheer numbers and actual and potential growth rates—something we will discuss momentarily—the issues confronting Canada are somewhat different. Canada's population, now and in the future, is relatively small given the immense size of the country, and this situation is not expected to change in any substantial way in the remaining decades of the twenty-first century. However, the fact that the natural rate of population growth in Canada has slowed considerably in recent years and is now close to zero while life expectancy has been steadily increasing is bound to have a major impact on the rate of economic growth, the viability of pension plans, and especially on immigration policies, including the number of immigrants Canada accepts each year.

This raises some important questions. How many immigrants and refugees should be admitted into Canada on a yearly basis? Is the current intake of approximately 250,000 immigrants per year too large or too small? What educational achievements, occupational skills, and linguistic capabilities should immigrants and refugees possess? What countries and parts of the world should future immigrants and refugees come from? Should immigrant and refugee policies and practices be based on economic interests, humanitarian concerns, or some judicious admixture of the two? Should immigrants and refugees be expected to live in specific parts of the country for certain periods of time, or should they be encouraged to settle wherever they like? While answers to these questions will have to be hammered out in the future, one thing is clear. A great deal of attention will need to be given to how many immigrants and refugees can be successfully integrated in the Canadian population and Canadian society each year and what educational and governmental programs as well as administrative procedures will be needed to ensure that this integration occurs with the least amount of friction and difficulty.

One final development should be discussed here before our attention is directed to the world situation as a whole. It is the impact of contemporary developments in communications, technology, and social media. There is no doubt that the world is being rapidly and radically transformed as a result of incredible developments in these areas. A shift of monumental proportions is occurring, one that is moving people and institutions out of a world predicated on verbal communications and the printed word and into a world predicated on virtual and visual reality and digital technology. Not only is this trend accelerating—some contend it is accelerating out of control—but also it is changing the way human beings interact with each other, interconnect, and live their lives.

Enormous benefits are being reaped as a result of these developments in all parts of Canada and throughout the world. Access to information, ideas, and the entire cultural heritage of humankind is expanding at a phenomenal rate. Through the Internet, people are able to visit every street, museum, and art gallery in the world, listen to the finest popular and classical music, see the greatest paintings and architecture, tour the world's most interesting towns, cities, and historic sites, and snap memorable photographs and share them instantly with friends and family.

Nevertheless, there is a downside to all this as well as an upside. Contemporary technology makes it increasingly difficult to maintain connections between people in human terms rather than merely on screen, as well as to keep neighbourhoods, communities, societies, and cultures intact. Everybody is so busy online that face-to-face contact and intimate interactions with family, friends, and neighbours are being eclipsed. As a result, people are becoming more self-absorbed, insular, and preoccupied, to the point that they are becoming insensitive to the needs and even the presence of others.

As one of the first and most "wired" nations in the world, Canada and its citizenry are in the forefront of many of today's technological developments. This means they are destined to play a powerful role in the development and use of these and other technological tools in the future. It is a role that will yield countless benefits, but also generate more than its share of problems if not dealt with successfully.

It is clear from all the changes taking place that the world is much more complex than it was in the past. Particularly disturbing is the fact that a matrix of global problems has emerged that appears to stand well beyond traditional solutions and structures. Without basic changes in the character and functioning of the world system as a whole, our planet could easily become a much more dangerous, demanding, and fragmented place.

Situated squarely in the middle of this matrix of global problems is the complex relationship people have with the natural environment. This involves far more than climate change and global warming, difficult though these matters are, since these issues are themselves embedded in a deeper, broader, and more demanding reality. Human beings are making colossal demands on the natural environment at the same time that the population of the world continues to increase rapidly. This is not a viable situation moving forward. In the first place, the way of life prevalent today in most parts of the world is highly materialistic and requires the consumption of natural resources at an enormous rate. In the second place, the natural environment was taken for granted and, in effect, ignored during the entire time the present world system was developing and gathering momentum during the eighteenth, nineteenth, and twentieth centuries. It is not possible to now insert the natural environment *after the fact* into this already existing way of life and world system. This is the biggest problem facing humanity and it would be foolhardy to diminish, deny, or ignore it.

Clearly, the more products are produced and consumed, the more construction and industrial development take place, the more trucks, vans, and cars appear on city streets, the more greenhouse gases and other forms of pollution are created and released into the atmosphere, the more the environment is degraded, and the more the global situation and world system deteriorate.

What makes this problem particularly acute is the fact that the world's population is already putting incredible stress on the world's finite carrying capacity. Matters will continue to worsen so long as people are unwilling to recognize this fact and make the changes in their values, behaviour, and ways of life necessary to set things right. Maintaining the status quo is no longer an option. *Things must change and change dramatically if the world and all the different countries in it are to become better rather than worse places in which to live and work.*

While it is difficult to predict with any certainty what the world's population will be by the end of the twenty-first century, there is no doubt that it will be substantially larger than it is today. Based on past experience, present trends, and future expectations, most experts estimate that the population of the world will grow from roughly 7½ billion people in 2017 to somewhere between 10 to 14 billion people by 2050 and possibly 16 to 18 billion people by the end of the century. Meanwhile, the carrying capacity of the earth will not have changed. In fact, if anything, it will have decreased, as arable land is degraded and resources consumed.

The ultimate consequences of this trend are predictable. As world population increases, there will be growing shortages of such basic necessities as water, grain, fish, arable land, and so forth. The prices of these necessities will rise considerably. We are already getting a taste of this, as prices for many natural resources, as well as basic foodstuffs such as fruits, vegetables, and meat, have increased significantly. As prices of basic staples increase, more tension, conflict, and hostility will be experienced throughout the world. This is not fear-mongering or attention-seeking. On the contrary, it is a realistic assessment of the present world situation and prospects for the future. These developments, coupled with increased inequalities in income and wealth, will heighten the demands for greater security, especially when this is considered in conjunction with the increased potential for terrorist attacks. The response to recent terrorist attacks in the U.S., France, and elsewhere in the world has given us a taste of what life will be like in the remaining decades of the twenty-first century if these problems are not addressed successfully and overcome.

While only three or four decades ago people were predicting a "borderless world," it is now clear that this will not be the case. Even with the most elaborate security procedures, crossing borders will take longer, threats to human life will be greater, and government scrutiny and surveillance will be more intense.

While Canada is better positioned to deal with these problems than most countries because of its munificent supply of natural resources and comparatively small population, this country is by no means immune to these problems, especially as the country's population is projected to increase to roughly 50 million by 2050 and possibly 70 million to 90 million by the end of the twenty-first century.

Given everything that we have discussed, the most important question facing all of us today, in Canada and around the world, is this: *How can a world system and overall way of life be created that makes it possible for **all** people and **all** countries to enjoy reasonable standards of living and a decent quality of life without straining the globe's scarce resources and finite carrying capacity to the breaking point?*

In order to achieve this, a very different type of world system and way of life will have to be created in the future. This system and way of life will have to prove capable of reducing the demands people are making on the natural environment, as well as dealing effectively with all the other problems that have loomed above the international horizon in recent years.

For Canada and Canadians, this means making a number of funda-mental changes in lifestyles, behaviour, attitudes, and actions. It also means participating actively in the quest to chart a new course for humanity.

Can the country and its citizenry achieve these goals and, in so doing, play an exemplary role in the world in the remaining years of the twenty-first century? Having considered Canada's past achievements and present situation, we are now in a perfect position to address this question.

CHAPTER SIX

Foundations for the Future

I f Canada's full potential is to be realized and Canadians are to play an exemplary role in the world, new foundations will have to be established for the future. This is because the foundations underlying the country's present system of development, like the foundations underlying the development of the entire world, are not sustainable.

Where do we commence the search for the building blocks necessary to create these foundations? Culture provides more than its fair share of possibilities, because it provides the breadth of vision and depth of understanding required to shed light on the way forward, especially when seen and dealt with in holistic terms.

For Canada and Canadians, this means developing Canadian culture in all its diverse aspects and manifestations. Canadians have worked incredibly hard over the centuries to build a culture that is capable of meeting the needs of the country's citizens for survival, material comfort, and general well-being. While the Canadian economy is an essential component of this, it is only one part of a substantially broader, deeper, and more fundamental process, namely Canadian culture *as a whole*. This is what accounts for Canada's high standard of living and superb quality of life, since it goes far beyond the country's economy to include many other activities and elements as well.

While up until now building Canadian culture has not been a conscious process, it must become one in the years ahead. Such deliberate forethought and action are necessary to make the changes that are required in the country's overall way of life in order to come to grips with the difficult problems confronting Canada and the world. Canadian culture in the all-encompassing sense should become the centrepiece and principal preoccupation of Canadian development in the remaining decades of the twenty-first century.

Considerable care must be exercised with respect to the way the term *culture* is used here and throughout this book. It is definitely not used in the nationalistic sense, since the nineteenth and twentieth centuries revealed that using the term in this way can result in excessive chest-thumping, military marching, the use of cultural symbols for exploitative purposes, suppression of some cultures by others, the assertion of cultural superiorities and inferiorities, and, in its most extreme and dangerous form, the killing of millions of people.

On the contrary, the term culture—and specifically Canadian culture—is used here in the all-inclusive sense to mean the way *in its entirety* that Canadians see and interpret the world, organize themselves, conduct their affairs, elevate and embellish life, and position themselves in the world. As such, it is concerned with the way *as a whole* in which Canadians live their lives and work out their complex association with the world. This is consistent with the way in which many anthropologists use the term culture to mean "the total way of life of a people," as well as why the well-known Quebec sociologist Fernand Dumont said, "I have always considered a collective project as something mainly cultural. The economy is not an end in itself, culture is."*

Canadian culture is made up of many different elements when it is conceived and dealt with in this way. In the first place, it takes in all the diverse activities that Canadians are engaged in as they go about the process of meeting their individual and collective needs. This includes all economic, commercial, technological, political, and educational activities as well as all artistic, scientific, recreational, athletic, spiritual, and other pursuits. In the second place, it includes the cultures of all the various ethnic groups that constitute the Canadian population. It also includes the cultures of all the geographical units—towns, cities, provinces, territories, and regions—that make up Canada.

This is what makes Canadian culture a dynamic and organic whole. Surely it is culture in this sense that Mahatma Gandhi was thinking of when he said, "A nation's culture resides in the hearts and in the soul of its people." National cultures—such as Canadian culture—are wholes that are greater than the sum of the parts. They consist of all the tangible and intangible elements that constitute them, as well as the ordering process used to combine those elements into a comprehensive whole.

To say that Canadian culture is a dynamic and organic whole is not to say that it is uniform or homogeneous, especially when nothing could be

---

* Bernard Ostry, *The Cultural Connection* (Toronto: McClelland and Stewart, 1978), p. 160.

farther from the truth. For the fact of the matter is that the country's culture is extremely diverse, much as the country's natural environment and population are. In cultural terms, this can be traced back to the Quebec Act of 1774, as indicated earlier, when a commitment was made to accepting and accommodating cultural differences between the French and the English rather than promoting subjugation and assimilation. Not only has this resulted in the creation of countless cultures in Canada that are distinct in their composition and character—such as the cultures of Quebec and Newfoundland and Labrador, Victoria, Winnipeg, and Charlottetown, and Indigenous and Japanese Canadians, to cite only a few examples—but also it has necessitated numerous concessions and compromises. While all these cultures are cultures in their own right, they are also integral parts of Canadian culture as a whole, which is why the country's culture is often described as a "mosaic" rather than a "melting pot."

Seen from this perspective, the central challenge facing Canada and Canadians in the future is to develop Canadian culture in all its diverse forms and manifestations, as well as to make the changes that are essential in the country's culture to come to grips with the newly emerging Canadian and global reality discussed earlier. In order to do this, Canadian culture will have to be positioned properly in the natural, historical, and global environment, and balanced and harmonious relationships will have to be established among all the diverse parts that make it up. Doing so will place the country and its citizenry in the strongest possible position to deal effectively with climate change and other aspects of the environment crisis, as well as come to grips with all the other problems that we face.

Heading the list of requirements in this regard is the need to position Canadian culture properly in the natural environment. Nothing is more important, since the natural environment provides the sustenance and wherewithal required to ensure the survival and meet the material needs of Canadians.

The fundamental importance of this was foreseen many years ago by two highly creative scholars from the University of British Columbia, William Rees and Mathis Wackernagel, when they developed the concept of the "ecological footprint." This remarkable idea, which has since been adopted and refined by many environmentalists, environmental organizations, academics, and governmental departments and agencies, is designed to show in concrete and specific terms how much of the natural environment is required to support human life in both the individual and collective sense.

There are two interrelated dimensions to the idea of the ecological footprint. In an individual sense, every person makes numerous *demands* on the natural environment and nature's resources as a result of his or her need for food, clothing, shelter, transportation, communications, energy, and so forth. They also *excrete* a great deal back into the natural environment in the form of garbage and waste. And what is true in the individual sense is also true in the collective sense. Every country, citizenry, economy, and culture, including Canada, Canadians, the Canadian economy, and Canadian culture, imposes an ecological footprint on the natural environment by consuming natural resources on the one hand and expelling wastes back into that environment on the other.

It was but a short step from this to the creation and development of scientific forms of measurement that could determine with remarkable accuracy the actual ecological footprint of people and countries. An individual's footprint, for instance, is ascertained by estimating the land area required in a variety of different categories to support a person's level of consumption using existing technologies. In the Canadian case, two-thirds of this footprint is accounted for by energy consumption, such as heating, lighting, air conditioning, and transportation, and by what is needed to produce, promote, and consume the goods and services that are required to satisfy the present standard of living and way of life of Canadians as individuals.

The average Canadian is estimated to consume roughly 850,000 kilojoules of energy every day. In consequence, the average Canadian requires approximately 4.8 hectares—that is to say, an area equivalent to about three city blocks—to support his or her total consumption habits and requirements over the course of a lifetime. While this large number results partly from the fact that Canadians live in a cold climate and need to consume more energy than people living in many other parts of the world, if every person in the world produced an ecological footprint as large as the average Canadian's, *it is estimated that it would take a world three times the present size to provide all the resources that are required to realize this.* In other words, Canada and Canadians are making an ecological footprint on the natural environment and world's resources in the collective sense that is not sustainable in the future in terms of the actual size and resources of the planet.

It follows from this that a new environmental reality is imperative that will dramatically alter the relationship Canadians have with the natural environment, and with this, the ecological footprint they impose in the future on the country's natural environment and scarce resources. The country and its citizenry can play a valuable role here not only in local, regional, and national terms, but also internationally. If Canada and Canadians can show that one of the world's largest per capita consumers of natural resources can transform present consumption practices and energy demands and create a very different type of relationship with the natural environment in the years and decades ahead, they will provide an excellent example for people and countries in other parts of the world. This will not be possible, however, without making a substantial change in the way of life that exists in Canada at present.

Think about what a powerful message this could send to people and countries in other parts of the world and the world as a whole. If Canada, which is probably better equipped to deal with the environmental crisis than any other country in the world in view of the country's huge size, abundant resources, and comparatively small population, can make a change of this magnitude, it could put the entire world on a path towards achieving the equilibrium that is necessary between the world's rapidly expanding population on the one hand and its finite carrying capacity on the other hand.

If the country's culture should be properly positioned in the natural environment, it should also be properly positioned in the historical environment. In other words, it should be properly positioned in time as well as in space.

History has a very important role to play here. Nothing starts from scratch and everything builds on everything else, which is why Marshall McLuhan said we see the future "through a rear-view mirror." Without a good understanding of the country's past—and with this the historical development of the country's culture, values, lifestyles, and way of life in terms of people, families, communities, neighbourhoods, creativity, diversity, peace, order, good government, caring, sharing, cooperation, and so forth—it will not be possible to create new foundations for the future.

This should not be taken to mean that Canadians should be dominated by the past or thoughts of the past. If Canadians are to face the future with optimism and enthusiasm rather than pessimism and anxiety, it is necessary to create the new values, lifestyles, customs, attitudes, behaviours, and overall way of life that are required for this, and therefore "think outside the box." Since the world of the future will be very different than the world of the present and the past—with many more risks, dangers, and uncertainties as well as many more rewards, benefits, and opportunities— thinking imaginatively and creatively about the future is imperative.

Nevertheless, whenever the future is contemplated, the first question should always be: what does the past, and especially development of the country's culture and historical values and ideals in the past, have to teach us that is relevant to the development of Canadian culture in the future? How did past generations of Canadians deal with similar problems, possibilities, and prospects? What insights, knowledge, information, ideas, wisdom, and understanding did they possess and what mistakes did they make that are pertinent to present and future generations and therefore helpful in thinking about the future and preparing properly for it?

Canada's response to the war on terrorism and the invasion of Iraq provide excellent examples of the relevance of the past to the future. When Canada and Canadians joined the war on terrorism after the terrorist attacks on United States on September 11, 2001, it was because terrorism is inconsistent with the country's values, ideals, culture, way of life, and historical development. Terrorism is morally wrong, ethically irresponsible, and an assault on human dignity and decency. As a result, there was never any question that Canada would become actively engaged in the war on terrorism, or that Canadians would commit the military personnel and financial resources that were required to fight terrorism. Involvement in this war—and the hunt for terrorists—was, is, and always will be consistent with Canada's historical development, traditions, and commitment to peace, security, freedom, and democracy. It is the same commitment that explains why Canada and Canadians became instantly and actively involved in the two world wars.

However, a very different dynamic was at work when Canada was asked to participate in the invasion of Iraq, and more recently, the bombing of Daesh (also known as ISIS or ISIL) targets and strongholds following the attacks in France, Germany, and other parts in the world. Although opinions varied markedly across the country at that time—many Canadians were in favour of joining the United States and other countries in the invasion of Iraq and attacks on Daesh targets and strongholds while many others were opposed—the federal government decided not to participate because this was contrary to Canada's history, values, and ideals. If conclusive proof could have been provided that Saddam Hussein was harbouring weapons of mass destruction, Canada would have joined the invasion of Iraq. However, since proof was not forthcoming, the federal government decided not to commit Canadian troops to this war.

This decision, which irked many Americans and Canadians at the time and demonstrated the price that has to be paid for leadership in the international arena, was consistent with the culture Canadians have built up over the centuries and enjoy today. It was also consistent with the Canadian constitution, as well as the will and interests of most Canadians. It was not in the cards for Canada and Canadians to participate in the invasion of Iraq or the later bombings of Daesh targets and strongholds until all avenues for peace were explored and alternative forms of engagement identified and developed, including training of local personnel on location and on the ground.

As these examples indicate, Canada's history, values, and ideals have a major role to play in ensuring that Canadian culture is properly positioned in the historical environment. Asking how previous generations of Canadians and especially the country's leaders dealt with the issues they faced—including both their achievements and what role they played in such matters as the establishment of prejudicial immigration policies and practices, the creation of residential schools, and other developments—is of vital importance in resolving these matters and making effective decisions about the future. These questions should always be asked, and careful consideration should be given to the answers before final decisions are made and specific courses of action taken.

Equally important in positioning Canadian culture properly in the historical environment is the need to address specific problems that have occurred in the past that have festered for generations and even centuries. This includes the injustices done to the Indigenous peoples, the Métis, and other minority and ethnic groups in Canada. This is why the various "truth and reconciliation" commissions that have been conducted in recent years are so valuable and important, as well as why actions in this area by the country's governments at every level are so essential. While significant strides have been made in coming to grips with these injustices, this process should be sustained and intensified in the future. There is still a long way to go before it will be possible to claim that the country's culture is properly situated in the historical environment (or time) as well as in the natural environment (or space).

To this must be added the need to situate the country's culture properly in the global environment, the third requirement if new foundations are to be laid for the future. This requirement is especially important if Canada and Canadians are to play the role they are capable of playing in the world of the future and realize their full potential in international as well as in domestic terms.

In order to achieve this, Canadians will have to get "square to the world" in much the same way that goalkeepers in hockey must get "square to the puck" if they are to perform effectively in the net. This means seeing the world clearly, objectively, impartially, and independently. Unfortunately, this is complicated by the fact that Canada is located next door to the most powerful nation on earth. This has a profound impact on every aspect and dimension of life and living in Canada, as Pierre Elliott Trudeau highlighted many years ago in his remark about living next door to an elephant and being affected by every movement it makes.

This is best illustrated in relation to Canadian defence policy. At the present time, the country's defence policy is so intimately tied up with the defence policy of the United States that it is virtually impossible to see Canada's requirements and posture clearly and separately from those of the U.S. Pressure is being exerted on Canada to commit to a single North American defence policy that would be directed largely by the United States. Matters are further complicated by the fact that Canada relies heavily on the United States to look after many of its most important military requirements, about which more will be said later.

This situation makes it difficult to determine what Canada's defence policy and requirements should be in the future, including what threats exist and what is required to protect the country and its citizenry from external attacks and aggression. It also makes it difficult to determine what defence plans and policies should be worked out in cooperation with United States—especially in regard to terrorist attacks, activities, and threats—and what policies should be pursued independently of the U.S. If Canada and its role in the world are to be seen clearly and objectively and Canada is to "get square to the world," it will be necessary to come to grips with this problem, even if this means paying the real (and likely much higher) cost of Canada's defence necessities in the years and decades ahead.

As this example illustrates, a whole set of issues exists where it will be necessary for Canadians to determine what is in their best interests in terms of global development and international affairs and how these matters can be dealt with most effectively. We are not only talking about defence policy here, but also trade policy, economic policy, monetary and fiscal policy, political policy, environmental policy, and many other policies with international implications and consequences.

There is no doubt that situating Canadian culture properly in the global environment will be affected by globalization and Canada's commitment to multiculturalism, as well as by the multiracial and multilingual character of the Canadian population. With more people coming to Canada from Asia, Africa, Latin America, the Caribbean, and the Middle East, Canadians are increasingly exposed to the needs, problems, and circumstances of people and countries in those parts the world. This augers well for the future because it provides a more balanced and comprehensive way of looking at and understanding the world.

Canadians will have to work extremely hard to be exposed to a variety of viewpoints from different parts of the world if these advantages are to be realized. This is particularly important with respect to the media—television, newspapers, and a variety of Internet and social media sources, sites, platforms, and networks—since the country's population receives most of its information from these sources and that information in turn affects attitudes towards the world and Canada's role and responsibilities in it. The federal government, including the Canadian Radio-television and Telecommunications Commission (CRTC), and Canada's various media organizations have a strategic role to play here. Canada simply cannot afford to allow greater concentration of media ownership to diminish Canadians' exposure to other news sources, viewpoints, and "takes on the world." The objective should be to create *Canadian* perspectives on the world that are authentic, impartial, and informed by attitudes, voices, and opinions from all parts of the world and not just the United States and Europe.

While it is difficult to predict political changes in the world with any accuracy or certainty, many think the promotion of democracy, which was a driving force in the late twentieth century, will diminish in importance and strength in the twenty-first century. This is because the United States seems to be losing interest in trying to promote democracy as it attempted to do during the George W. Bush administration early in the century. This has resulted in the emergence of a multipolar rather than unipolar world, with many more countries, such as China, Russia, and India, vying for power and influence.

Canada could play a valuable role here through its ability to work cooperatively with other nations, peoples, and institutions, as well as its capacity to play a conciliatory rather than aggressive or assertive role in the world. Canadians understand the need to achieve "unity in diversity" better than most due to the country's historical and contemporary development and experiences with multiculturalism and pluralism. They also understand the need to pursue policies that are peaceful rather than provocative, collaborative rather than confrontational, multilateral rather than unilateral. Not only was Canada the first western nation to recognize the People's Republic of China, but it also played a valuable role in assisting Ethiopia with its famine and drought, as well as an important role in bringing apartheid and the apartheid regime to an end in South Africa.

When all these diverse factors and forces are combined and considered collectively, it is clear that Canada must expand its international activities and role in the world very considerably in the future and do so *on its own terms*. Not only will this rectify the serious imbalance that exists at present between Canada's internal and external development, but also it will make it possible for the country and its citizenry to play a much stronger and more distinct role in the world, while at the same time taking advantage of many economic, social, technological, political, humanitarian, and other opportunities that exist throughout the world.

An understanding of Canada and its role in the world of the future must be forged that focuses on what Canada, Canadians, and Canadian culture have to give *to* the world and not only on what they have to gain *from* the world. This includes contributions to peace, security, sustainable development, environmental preservation and protection, foreign aid and developmental assistance, international trade, overcoming huge disparities in income and wealth, resolving long-standing disputes, disagreements, and grievances between the diverse peoples, cultures, religions, and civilizations of the world, and coming to grips with terrorism. These are the tough and demanding issues that will have to be addressed and dealt with effectively if Canadian culture is to be properly positioned in the global environment in the remaining decades of the twenty-first century.

If it is necessary to situate Canadian culture properly in the global, historical, and natural environment as new foundations are laid for the future, it is equally essential to achieve balance and harmony between the many diverse components that constitute the country's culture.

This is without doubt one of the greatest strengths of seeing and dealing with Canadian culture *as a whole*. It is a strength that is missing in the world today. On the one hand, it makes it possible to focus on the disharmonies and imbalances that exist between component parts of the country's culture, such as those between the material and non-material dimensions of development, between the public sector and the private sector, the arts and the sciences, rich and poor Canadians, technology and society, and so forth. On the other hand, it makes it possible to see clearly what course of action should be taken in the future to overcome these disharmonies and imbalances. This simply can't be achieved without taking a holistic and impartial, rather than partial and partisan, approach to the development of Canadian culture, since the emphasis in the latter case is always on the parts and not on the whole.

The Dutch cultural scholar, Johan Huizinga, gave us a profound insight into one of the most important of these disharmonies or imbalances and how it can be confronted and overcome. It is the disharmony or imbalance that exists between the material and non-material or quantitative and qualitative dimensions of development. This disharmony or imbalance not only affects Canada and Canadians, but the world as a whole. It simply must be confronted and overcome if humanity is to reduce the colossal demands it is making on the natural environment, the world's scarce resources, and the finite carrying capacity of the earth.

After examining many cultures, countries, and civilizations in the world, Huzinga stated that "the realities of economic life, of power, of technology, of everything conductive to man's material well-being must be balanced by strongly developed spiritual, intellectual, moral, and aesthetic values." The power and profundity of this statement is revealed through its remarkable relevance to the present and prospective situation in Canada and elsewhere in the world.

This insight has major implications for the development of Canada and Canadian culture in the future. A much higher priority will have to be placed on artistic, ethical, humanistic, educational, and spiritual activities in the overall development of Canada and Canadian culture in the years and decades ahead if the aforementioned disharmony is to be overcome and a better balance achieved.

The benefits that would be derived from this would be enormous. This is because achieving and maintaining a balance of this type would substantially decrease the demands Canadians are making on the natural environment and country's natural resources, since artistic, ethical, educational, humanistic, and spiritual activities are largely labour-intensive rather than material- or capital-intensive and consequently don't draw as heavily on the resources of nature as the large majority of economic, commercial, and technological activities. This would provide one of the best solutions of all to the environmental crisis, especially as the Canadian population increases and more pressure is exerted on the natural environment and country's natural resource legacy.

This "environmental imperative" will require a major shift away from the stimulation and satisfaction that comes from materialism, the marketplace, and the consumption of "stuff" to the fulfillment that comes from intellectual, ethical, artistic, humanistic, and spiritual activity. Not only would this make it possible for Canadians to "walk more lightly on the land," but also it is the only real hope for a planet that is rapidly approaching the limits of its natural-resource base and carrying capacity.

This would also make it possible for a significant percentage of the Canadian population of all ages, types, stages in life, and living in all parts of the country to enjoy much more fulfillment in life. It is no coincidence in this respect that there is a great deal of talk these days about "cultural creatives." These are people who are not finding the fulfillment, meaning, and significance they are searching for in life through materialism, consumerism, and the marketplace, and who are therefore looking for more contentment and pleasure in other ways. The key to this—as many Canadians and people in other parts of the world are beginning to discover—lies to achieving a better balance between materialism and spiritualism and the quantitative and qualitative dimensions of life. This often ranks very high whenever Canadians are polled about their needs and desire to create more fulfilling lifestyles and ways of life for themselves.

This will not be possible as long as "wealth" is seen and treated the way it currently is in Canada. Clearly wealth is defined largely in terms of income, money, and materialism. To be a wealthy person is to be a person who possesses a great deal of money, income, and material possessions, or has access to them or control over them. This focuses much more attention on "quantity of life" than "quality of life." However, when wealth is viewed from a broader, deeper, and more fundamental cultural or holistic perspective, the qualitative dimension comes to the fore. Wealth in this sense, as Huizinga rightly observed, means achieving an effective balance between all the different factors, forces, and activities that constitute life, culture, and development.

We are talking about *well-being* here rather than *wealth* in the conventional sense. While concern with creating wealth in financial and material terms has dominated Canadian development over much of the last two centuries, concern with well-being should drive Canadian development in the future. This is yet another reason why cultivating Canadian culture fully and effectively in the future is a categorical imperative.

Huizinga's remarkable insight into this matter also provides the key to making some basic changes in the Canadian economy and the way it is structured in the future. In order to realize this, it is necessary to situate the country's economy in a comprehensive cultural context, as well as imbue it with many more artistic, ethical, humanistic, educational, and spiritual dimensions than is the case at present. Not only will this help to position the Canadian economy properly in Canadian culture—and with it the natural, historical, and global environment—but it will also humanize the country's economy to a much greater extent. It will also make the economy more sensitive to the need to treat people with dignity, compassion, and respect, thereby placing a great deal more emphasis on caring, sharing, cooperation, inclusion, and equality, and consequently more equitable distributions of income and wealth. It will likewise yield new forms and types of economic activity—forms and types that are cleaner, greener, shared, creative, and entrepreneurial, as well as more in keeping with the needs of future generations of Canadians.

If achieving a better balance between the material and non-material or quantitative and qualitative dimensions of life in Canada is one benefit to be derived from seeing and treating Canadian culture as a whole and seeking balance and harmony among its many different parts, so is dealing with many other imbalances and disharmonies that exist throughout the country. This is particularly true with respect to the imbalances or disharmonies that exist between the public sector and private sector and rich and poor Canadians, matters which will be addressed in detail in the chapters to follow.

Suffice it to say here that each of these matters will have to be dealt with effectively and overcome in the remaining decades of the twenty-first century. So, too, will many injustices and inequalities, especially those having to do with income, employment, ethnicity, race, gender, people, and the various regions of the country. For this is what seeing and dealing with Canadian culture as a whole and endeavouring to achieve balance and harmony among its many different parts is all about. It is about achieving equilibrium between all the diverse activities, causes, concerns, and components that constitute the country's culture. While this is an idealistic goal that is exceedingly difficult to achieve in fact, it is worthy of pursuit because it will lead to more equality, inclusion, and sustainability in Canada's cultural life. This is primarily because the cultural or holistic approach places much more emphasis on people, human welfare, and environmental well-being than it does on products, profits, materialism, and the bottom line. This change in perspective could lead to significant improvements in the way Canadians deal with climate change, the environmental crisis, homelessness, poverty, child care, affordable housing, foreign aid, developmental assistance, the north, and a host of other issues and concerns.

When the World Commission on Environment and Development produced its report *Our Common Future* in 1982, it singled out "sustainable development" as *the* most important requirement for the world of the future. This served as a wake-up call for people and countries in all parts of the world. It emphasized the fact that people cannot go on acting as if it is "business as usual," pursuing ways of life that fail to take into account the natural environment, other species, future generations, and the poorest and most destitute peoples and countries of the world in developmental planning, policy, and decision-making. What is true for the world in general is also true for Canada and Canadians in particular if they are to thrive and prosper in the twenty-first century and play the role they are capable of playing in the world.

At its most fundamental and foundational level, this means developing a culture in the country that is sustainable, humane, equitable, and inclusive rather than unsustainable, inhumane, inequitable, and exclusive. Not only should this culture—Canadian culture—have a rich vein of creativity, diversity, vitality, and unity flowing through it, but also it should include all the diverse activities and cultures that comprise this culture and meld them together in such a way that it is a harmonious whole shared by all Canadians, rather than a smorgasbord of disconnected and unrelated parts.

Having established what Canadian culture should be like in this idealistic and holistic sense, the time has come to direct our attention to how this can be achieved in practical, concrete, and operational terms.

CHAPTER SEVEN

A New Political and Public Reality

I t is one thing to make Canadian culture the centrepiece and principal preoccupation of Canadian development in the idealistic and
holistic sense. It is quite another to achieve this in fact.

In both historical and contemporary terms, development of Canadian
culture in the holistic sense has been seen and treated as a *consequence* of
other developments rather than a development in its own right. As a
result, the focus has been on developing specific parts of Canadian
culture—agriculture, industry, education, politics, and government in
earlier periods and the economy more recently—rather than on developing
Canadian culture as a whole. In consequence, the country's culture has
been viewed and treated as an afterthought and a "residual activity," and
therefore in a passive rather than active way. It is going to take a quantum
leap in Canadian consciousness to see and treat the development of Canadian culture in a proactive, deliberate, systematic, and comprehensive
manner.

In order to achieve this, it will be necessary in the future to deal with
Canadian culture in much the same way that the Canadian economy has
been dealt with over much of the last century and especially over the last
fifty years, namely as the centrepiece and principal preoccupation of
Canadians and Canadian development. The most important question
would no longer be what is in the best interests of the Canadian economy—essential as this is—but, rather, what is in the best interests of
Canadian culture *as a whole*. This has major implications for Canada,
Canadians, and Canadian development in general, and for the public
sector, the private sector, and the relationship between these two sectors
in particular, in the remaining decades of the twenty-first century.

While all Canadians and all Canadian organizations have an important
role to play in the development of Canadian culture in practical and concrete terms, from where should the initial and main thrust come to set this
process in motion and ensure that it is steered in the right direc-

tion? Should it come from corporations, citizens, community groups, governments, towns, cities, the provinces and territories, the diverse regions of the country, or somewhere else?

There are two very compelling reasons why it should come from the public sector in general and governments and the political process in particular. In the first place, the public sector, governments, and the political process share a great deal in common with culture in general and Canadian culture in the holistic sense in particular. While their basic objectives are not the same—the former are concerned largely with law, order, stability, security, peace, and good government whereas the latter are concerned primarily with creativity, excellence, diversity, people's experiences, and the quest for the sublime—there is one area where they share an enormous amount in common *in principle* if not always in practice. It is the need to see the "big picture" and not just specific parts of it, as well as to achieve balance and harmony between the various parts of the big picture.

This is one of the highest goals of the public sector, governments, governance, and the political process in most if not all parts of the world, just as it is one of the highest goals of culture, cultures, and Canadian culture in the all-inclusive sense. While governments, politics, and the political process in Canada and other parts of the world have lost sight of this goal in the modern era—largely by getting so caught up in specific parts of the big picture—there is no doubt that this goal remains one of their most fundamental concerns, regardless of whether they are socialist, liberal, or conservative in character.

But there is another, equally compelling reason why the country's public sector, governments, and the political process should take the lead in setting this process in motion and ensuring that it is steered in the right direction. If they do not assume this role, the development of Canadian culture in proactive, deliberate, systematic, and comprehensive terms *will not occur at all in the concrete and practical sense.* This is because all other individuals, institutions, and activities in Canada—regardless of how important or powerful they are or may become—are concerned with specific *parts* of Canadian culture, not Canadian culture *as a whole.*

As essential as corporations, foundations, scientific, artistic, and athletic organizations, health and welfare agencies, citizens' coalitions, and so forth are, and no matter how much they contribute to the development of Canadian culture, their principal concern and preoccupation is not with Canadian culture as a whole but rather with specific parts of it, such as addressing particular needs, contributing to worthwhile causes, producing goods and services, creating artistic and scientific works, developing recreational and athletic activities, and so forth. While these are all essential activities, they are concerned with parts of Canadian culture and not culture in the all-inclusive sense.

This is why Canada's public sector, governments, and political process have a proactive and leadership role to play—rather than a reactive and passive role—in making Canadian culture the centrepiece of the country's development in the years ahead. It is essential for the country's governments to be fully engaged in this process, particularly the federal government since it is concerned with Canadian culture in all its many diverse aspects and manifestations, as well as from a national and international perspective.

What are some of the initial steps that should be taken by the country's governments and especially the federal government to perform this role effectively? Consistent with the foundations for the future discussed earlier, the most essential requirement of all is creating a new relationship between Canadians and the natural environment.

In practical terms, this means ensuring that three things are done and done extremely well: cleaning up the natural environment whenever and wherever necessary; ensuring the conservation of natural resources and reducing carbon emissions and those of other pollutants; and increasing people's awareness of the sanctity, profundity, and fragility of the country's natural environment. While ultimately all Canadians and all Canadian institutions have an important stake in this matter, the country's governments and especially the federal government will have to play the leading role if these three interlocking requirements are to be met.

The first requirement requires numerous actions designed to eliminate toxic substances, as well as to develop sound and sustainable environmental policies, practices, and systems. The second requirement involves many additional measures, such as achieving and increasingly exceeding the targets agreed to during and after the Paris Conference of 2015 with respect to climate change and reductions in the use of fossil fuels. It also requires phasing out the use of coal; rigorously enforcing standards with respect to carbon emissions and carbon pricing agreements; purifying water and air and protecting water as the most vital resource of all; developing alternative forms of energy such as wind and solar power and fuel-cell and electric technology; making more and better use of public transit; and changing the time-scale and space-scale of products so that they don't wear out as easily, last longer, are recycled at every opportunity, and don't require as many resources to produce in the first place. While the country's governments need not be directly involved in all these matters in the operational sense, they should act to ensure that they are carried out by the many public and private sector individuals and institutions responsible for them.

As important as the first two requirements are, the third requirement is the most essential of all. It requires the creation and cultivation of very different lifestyles, attitudes, and behaviours with respect to the country's natural environment and Canadians' interactions with it—ones based on treating the natural environment as a spiritual entity that deserves reverence and respect rather than depletion, domination, and exploitation. The Indigenous peoples have a great deal to contribute here as they have developed environmental policies, practices, principles, and lifestyles that manifest keen insights into what is required to live in harmony with nature, other species, and "the land." It is re-assuring in this respect to know that Natural Resources Canada recently awarded contracts to the North Slave Métis Alliance and the government of the Ticho First Nation to study traditional and cultural knowledge concerned with climate change and environmental interaction in the Northwest Territories. Let's hope this is the first of many similar developments and commitments in the future.

What is true for the Indigenous peoples is also true for the country's artists. Many Canadian artists draw heavily on nature and the natural environment in the creation and development of their works. Some of the most obvious examples are visual artists such as Tom Thomson, Emily Carr, the Group of Seven, Doris McCarthy, and Robert Bateman, authors such as Farley Mowat, Margaret Atwood, Graeme Gibson, Ernest Thompson Seton, Grey Owl, and Wade Davis, and composers such as Violet Archer, Harry Freedman, Jean Papineau-Couture, Harry Somers, and R. Murray Schafer. Not only do their works bring many aspects of the natural environment across the country to our attention, but they also enhance our understanding of why it is so important to protect the country's natural environment and revere it as the most essential resource of all.

What is true for the natural environment and its conservation is equally true for the country's cultural heritage, which is also an integral and indispensable part of the development of Canadian culture. This is especially important for the country's museums, libraries, art galleries, and archival institutions, as noted earlier because they store most of the visual and verbal records, documents, materials, and memorabilia that connect Canadians to their past and bind Canada and Canadian culture together in space and time, thereby providing a strong sense of national identity, unity, and purpose.

Seen from this perspective, reports by the Auditor General of Canada, Library and Archives Canada, and other heritage institutions have in recent years painted a disturbing picture of the state of Canada's cultural heritage and its most important custodial and conservation institutions. It is a picture of eroding facilities, equipment, and infrastructure at the federal, provincial/territorial, and municipal levels.

While a strong system of political and governmental support for the country's cultural heritage was developed in the 1970s under the leadership of Gérard Pelletier when he was Secretary of State, unfortunately this system has since deteriorated because of funding cuts and preoccupation with other priorities, programs, policies, and problems. As a result, the country is not being served to best advantage by its cultural heritage at a time when this is required more than ever to counteract strong pressures from the United States, strengthen Canadian identity, and deal effectively with globalization and the demands of a troubled and increasingly volatile planet.

A strong commitment to heritage conservation on the part of the country's governments would go a long way towards rectifying this problem. So, too, would acquainting Canadians more fully with Canada's historical values, customs, traditions, and overall way of life if experiences in many European countries and other parts of the world are a guide, especially with respect to the need for greater integration, interaction, orientation, and education with respect to all the various peoples, groups, and cultures that exist in Canada. While physical infrastructure such as roads, railroads, highways, airports, bridges, and so forth are important and deserve a high priority, so do the country's libraries, museums, archives, art galleries, and other custodial institutions.

If improving the country's environmental situation and heritage system is imperative if Canadian culture is to be developed effectively in practical terms, so is coming to grips with many other matters that are of utmost importance. Included here, as indicated earlier, are treating the Indigenous peoples and Métis with respect, bringing Quebec fully into the Canadian family, and helping marginalized and oppressed groups. While Canada has made a great deal of progress in recent years in a number of these areas, there is no doubt that improving the treatment of Indigenous peoples, implementing the recommendations contained in the Truth and Reconciliation Report and other major documents, speeding up the settlement of land claims and treaty agreements, addressing the killing and raping of Indigenous women, dealing with the legacy of the residential schools, coming to grips with many other historical injustices and grievances, and resolving the present impasse between Quebec and the rest of Canada would go a long way towards developing Canadian culture in practical and concrete terms.

If the country's governments and especially the federal government have a leadership role to play in shifting the focus of decision-making to Canadian culture as a whole, they also have a leadership role to play in achieving parity between the economic and non-economic dimensions of the country's culture. The key to achieving this change in concrete terms lies, as noted earlier, in making the fundamental shift from *wealth* to *well-being*. Well-being goes beyond our current preoccupation with materialism and economic growth to deal with the need to create a greatly improved *quality of life* through better health and physical fitness, more reliable and fulfilling jobs, more viable communities and neighbourhoods, stimulating possibilities for rest, relaxation, and revitalization, development of a positive outlook on life, and much more.

It is impossible for governments to play a leadership role in this area without getting deeply immersed in matters of citizenship. While the country's governments and citizens will always be concerned with countless economic, financial, and commercial matters—this will never change—such matters should not be their immediate or ultimate concern. The highest priority should be to empower citizens to live happy, healthy, creative, constructive, and fulfilling lives.

While concern with citizens' rights has been a principal preoccupation over the last seven or eight decades, as evidenced by the United Nations' Universal Declaration of Human Rights (1948) and the Canadian Charter of Rights and Freedoms (1982), much more consideration should be given to citizens' *responsibilities* in all future definitions and understandings of Canadian citizenship. This is a fundamental prerequisite to making the transition from wealth to well-being.

Without doubt, the Universal Declaration and the Charter were remarkable achievements. While confirmation of these rights and freedoms was a valuable step forward, it should be accompanied in the future by the creation of a comparable set of Canadian responsibilities and what might be called a "Canadian Charter of Rights and Responsibilities." Of what do these responsibilities consist? Among countless other things, respect for nature and other species; reducing Canadians' huge ecological footprint; respect for existing Canadian customs, values, and worldviews as well as the creation and cultivation of new ones where necessary; acting in a responsible, cooperative, and conciliatory rather than aggressive and confrontational manner; learning as much as possible about Canadian culture and the various cultures that constitute that culture; pursuing peace, harmony, and unity rather than conflict, confrontation, and disunity; achieving and maintaining a high level of health and physical fitness; and helping others, including the less fortunate and needy here in Canada and around the world. These responsibilities are consistent with the need to take a cultural or holistic approach to Canadian citizenship because they are concerned with "the other" as well as "the self," with giving as well as taking, and with treating all Canadians and the natural environment with dignity and respect.

If the country's governments and especially the federal government have a powerful role to play in making decisions about a variety of practical, concrete, and operational matters like these, they also have a vital role to play in ensuring that appropriate indicators are developed to measure progress toward this goal. The key lies in developing a set of *comprehensive cultural indicators* that can be used to evaluate the overall state and status of Canadian culture, as well as the lives of Canadian citizens overall, not just their economic circumstances and material needs. This should constitute a basic practice and fundamental feature of all developmental activities and decision-making processes by Canadian governments in the future, especially when recent research has revealed that economic indicators such as per capita income and gross domestic product do not provide an accurate or adequate assessment of the real standard of living, quality of life, and state of well-being of Canadians because they deal with only one dimension of life, albeit an extremely important one.

This is an area where Canada is already manifesting a great deal of international leadership and playing a highly creative and pioneering role in the world, due largely to research undertaken in this area by a number of Canadian think tanks and policy institutes, including the Canadian Policy Research Networks, the Atkinson Foundation, and the University of Waterloo, among others. While the human development index and other indicators developed by the United Nations several decades ago represented an important step forward in this regard—largely by extending the notion of wealth beyond indicators such as income per capita, net domestic product, and the rate of economic growth to include indicators related to life expectancy and educational level—they do not take other factors into account that are equally essential in assessing the state of Canadian culture and the well-being of Canadians in the collective, public sense as well as the individual, personal sense.

In addition to the usual economic indicators referred to above, this set of comprehensive cultural indicators should include: *environmental indicators* such as the quality of water and air and levels of toxicity and waste; *health indicators* such as human longevity and the availability and effectiveness of health care systems and institutions; *social indicators* such as access to social assistance and support services as well as gender and racial equity; *educational indicators* such as pupil-teacher ratios, graduation rates, and access to elementary, secondary, post-secondary, and adult education; *political indicators* such as the stability and effectiveness of political institutions and governmental procedures and policies; *safety and security indicators* such as protection from terrorism and terrorist attacks; *recreational indicators* such as the availability of parks, conservation areas, and a variety of leisure-time activities; and *aesthetic and spiritual indicators* such as the quantity and quality of artistic offerings, the diversity of artistic, religious, and spiritual endeavours, and so forth.

Since many of these indicators already exist, the challenge of the future will be to pull all the existing indicators together and create any new ones that are necessary in order to form a comprehensive set of cultural indicators, as well as to rank all these indicators according to their actual importance in the overall scheme of things. This will make it possible to ascertain the state of Canadian culture and the general well-being of Canadians from a cultural and holistic perspective rather than a limited economic and financial perspective.

The closest form of measurement to this existing at the present time is the highly creative Canadian Index of Wellbeing (CIW) developed at the University of Waterloo and other locations over the last decade. While gross domestic product (GDP) is restricted to financial transactions throughout the Canadian economy, the CIW includes fluctuations in community activity and vitality, democratic engagement, education, environment, health, leisure activities and the arts, and living standards and time use, thereby providing a much more inclusive and extensive assessment of the well-being of Canadians.

According to CIW's most recent report, Canadians are falling behind in terms of well-being and have been doing so during much of the last decade. This is because improvements in the well-being of Canadian citizens have not kept pace with the modest increases that have been achieved in per capita income over the same time period, due largely to the spread of precarious and contract employment, longer commute and wait times, loss of leisure time, more unequal distribution of income, longer working hours, and so forth. This is why Roy Romanow, who has played a key role in the development of the CIW, declared, "The complex issues of our time require evidence, integrated systems thinking, and proactive approaches. As we set our course for the next 150 years, we need to place the well-being of Canadians at the very heart of Canada's vision."*

Much like cultural indicators, the arts and humanities have an essential role to play in making the transition from wealth to well-being in Canada. Not only are the arts primarily concerned with the needs, problems, and well-being of Canadian citizens, but they also broaden, deepen, and intensify participation in the country's culture and enjoyment of it. This is because Canadian artists create many of the signs, symbols, myths, legends, metaphors, and rituals required to enhance Canadians' well-being and expand their knowledge, awareness, and understanding of Canadian culture. They achieve this by deliberately choosing parts of the country's culture that are symbolic of the whole and using those parts as the principal themes and basic elements in their works.

Unfortunately, the same problem that exists with respect to the country's cultural heritage and custodial institutions exists with respect to the country's artists and artistic organizations. Many are perched precariously close to bankruptcy or collapse, facing countless financial hardships.

Canada's artists and artistic organizations deserve a much higher priority and considerably more funding from federal, provincial, and municipal governments if they are to fulfill their mandates as crucial contributors to the development of the country's culture and the well-being of Canadians. Substantially increasing the budgets of the CBC, NFB, the Canada Council for the Arts, the Department of Canadian Heritage, the Social Sciences and Humanities Research Council, and many other national organizations—and their counterpart organizations at the provincial, territorial, and municipal levels—would go a long way towards achieving the balance and parity that is required in this area. This is imperative if the arts and humanities are to flourish in Canada in the years and decades ahead.

*Roy Romanow, "Pursuit of economic growth is leaving millions behind," *Toronto Star*, November 22, 2016, p. A15.

Artistic and humanistic activities and organizations bring the country and its citizenry together in collective, human, and humane ways. They also create countless bonds and connections between Canadians, as well as opening up new vistas and opportunities that border on the beautiful, the inspirational, and the sublime. This comes at a time when many Canadians are searching for more happiness, fulfillment, spirituality, and well-being in life.

If the country's governments, and especially the federal government, provide the initial and main thrust in making Canadian culture the centrepiece and principal preoccupation of the country's development in practical and concrete terms, this should be expanded and enhanced substantially by other public sector organizations, activities, and initiatives. It is particularly important for the country's educational institutions to make a strong commitment to teaching and learning about Canadian culture in the holistic sense on a full-time and aggressive basis. Building on the example provided by the country's governments, the country's schools, colleges, and universities should take steps to ensure that studying and learning about Canadian culture in all its diverse aspects and manifestations—how it developed, where it stands at present, where it should be headed in the future, and how it functions as a whole—are addressed fully and situated at the core of the country's educational system. Not only should educational institutions delve far more intensively into this matter than they do today, but they should also design future courses, curricula, evaluative criteria, teacher training, and research projects with this end in mind.

This is especially important with respect to achieving a better balance between the quantitative and qualitative dimensions of Canadian culture, cultivating more commitment to environmental conservation, realizing equality in the educational system between the arts and humanities on the one hand and sciences and technology on the other, focusing more attention on physical education, fitness, and lifelong learning, and training students to play an active, responsible, and humane role in Canada and the world. This is about much more than procedures and priorities, essential as these are. More fundamentally, it is about transformation and change, especially in terms of dealing with these matters in sufficient breadth and depth so as to lead to the creation of new perceptions, ideas, ideals, lifestyles, values, and different ways of living for future generations of Canadians.

Two major benefits would result from this. In the first place, Canadians would realize that they share an enormous amount in common despite their differences. While Canadian educators have achieved remarkable results, the creation of a set of *national* values, objectives, priorities, courses, and standards has always eluded them (except in a few highly specialized areas) since education is a provincial rather than federal responsibility. Learning about Canadian culture in the holistic sense could solve this problem by focusing on common themes, values, and elements.

But there is another, equally essential benefit to be derived from teaching and learning about Canadian culture. It results from the fact that creativity lies at the very heart and soul of this culture. Consequently, learning about the historical and contemporary development of the country's culture has substantial implications for—and dramatically increases exposure to—the remarkable creativity of Canadians. As illustrated earlier, this creativity exists in every domain of the country's cultural life, from food, clothing, shelter, transportation, communications, and health care to the arts, sports, recreation, the sciences, and natural environment. As a result, it is an ideal way to tell the Canadian story, as well as learn about how creative Canadians actually are and have been over the centuries. This comes at a time when individuals and institutions in all parts of the country and the world are coming to the conclusion that creativity provides the wherewithal required to come to grips with many of Canada's and the world's most pressing, complex, persistent, and debilitating problems.

If teaching and learning about Canadian culture and creativity should be accorded a much higher priority in the country's educational system in the future, so should teaching and learning in the two "book-ends" of this system, namely early childhood education at one end and adult education at the other. Interestingly, Canadians have made seminal contributions in both these areas that are recognized around the world, particularly the contributions of Fraser Mustard to early childhood education and Roby Kidd to adult education.

Fraser Mustard was a tireless promoter of early childhood education in Canada and throughout the world. He was convinced that the first 2,000 days in a child's life—roughly from birth to the age of five or six—are of vital importance in terms of a person's ability to learn throughout life and therefore the key to their long-term development and well-being. There is now virtually unanimous agreement among educators everywhere in the world that children learn best and have the greatest potential for learning when they are very young, confirming the belief that formal education should start much sooner than it does at present. This is well-documented in the many reports Fraser Mustard wrote on this matter over the years, especially the *Early Years Study* he co-authored with Margaret McCain, the former Lieutenant-Governor of New Brunswick, for the Ontario government.

While Mustard was involved in the creation of many valuable activities and institutions in Canada—most notably the Faculty of Medicine at McMaster University and the Institute for Advanced Research in Toronto—one of his most important achievements was realized just before his death in 2014. It was the creation of the Institute for Human Development at the University of Toronto, which is committed to studying issues related not only to early childhood education and its impact on people's entire lives, but also to human development at all ages and stages and how it can be enhanced most effectively in the future.

What Fraser Mustard achieved at one end of the educational spectrum, Dr. Roby Kidd achieved at the other, almost half a century earlier. Kidd had an illustrious career in education in general and adult education in particular, both in Canada and throughout the world. It commenced with teaching adults at the YMCA in 1935, and included teaching the first adult education course in Canada at the University of British Columbia, serving as Chair of UNESCO's advisory committee on adult education after the Second World War, acting as director of the Canadian Association for Adult Education from 1951 to 1982, helping to found the International Association of Adult Education and lobbying to have its headquarters located in Canada, and writing a seminal book, *How Adults Learn* (1959), that has been translated into many languages.

Like Mustard, Kidd was totally committed to education, in this case educating adults who were either deprived of having any education at all or encouraging those who did to continue their studies after elementary or secondary school and indeed throughout life. As a result, he was a major contributor to the field now known as "lifelong learning" and "education for life," which involves education from the cradle to the grave.

Not only was this important in Kidd's view for practical purposes, such as securing employment, but also it was important for living a healthy, productive, and well-rounded life. This type of education involves not only enjoying and profiting from learning in early childhood as well as in the final stages of life, but also from developing and maintaining a good outlook throughout one's entire life. This should be a fundamental goal for all Canadian educational institutions, citizens, and governments.

If Canada's educational system has a seminal role with respect to the quintessential importance of Canadian culture in the country's development, this role should be extended and enhanced by other public sector institutions as well. There is a vast panorama of public sector institutions in every field of cultural endeavour throughout the country that need to be developed more fully and placed on a firmer financial foundation. The list is long, but then so too are the rewards, especially in terms of expanding the operations, research, outreach, and ability of these and other organizations to play a forceful role in the development of Canadian culture.

It is not difficult to see what is going on here. In the process of shifting the future focus of attention to the development of Canadian culture, the agenda would be driven much more by the public sector than by the private sector. This contrasts sharply with the past and present, when the highest priority has been accorded to the private sector. As a result, corporations have been afforded numerous opportunities and special privileges because they produce the material wealth required to fuel the Canadian economy, create many jobs, and make improvements in Canadians' material standard of living.

This system is breaking down. An increased percentage of the country's economic output is being produced by machines rather than by people as a result of phenomenal developments in technology and artificial intelligence. Moreover, countless jobs and employment opportunities are being lost or outsourced to other countries, and many Canadian corporations are holding on to their profits rather than investing them because they are more concerned with their financial requirements than the needs and interests of Canadian citizens and the country as a whole. This has necessitated more action by the country's governments to oversee and regulate the economy in the public interest and ensure that private-sector concerns and the preoccupations of corporations and financial institutions do not conflict with public-sector requirements, the public trust, and the needs of Canada, Canadian citizens, and Canadian culture as a whole.

All this is happening at a time when more problems in Canada and elsewhere in the world are being dealt with by the public sector. Think about it for a moment. What are the big problems facing Canada, Canadians, people and countries in other parts of the world, and the world as a whole today? While the Canadian economy, the economies of other countries, and the overall global economy continue to pose serious challenges, most of the principal issues and concerns confronting the country, its citizenry, people and countries in other parts of the world, and the world as a whole are public-sector issues and concerns.

The most obvious examples of this are the environmental crisis; the colossal demands people are making on the world's scarce resources and finite carrying capacity; the huge inequalities that exist in income and wealth throughout the world; the need for stepped-up safety and security procedures and for dealing effectively with terrorism and terrorists; conflicts between different groups, countries, races, and religions; and the need for much more public-sector infrastructure. And what is true at present will likely be even more true in the future.

Governments have a particularly important role to play in this. As David Orr, a well-known environmentalist and public policy specialist, pointed out in his book *Down to the Wire* in 2009:

> Only governments have the power to set the rules for the economy, enforce the law, levy taxes, ensure the fair distribution of income, protect the poor and future generations, cooperate with other nations, negotiate treaties, defend the public interest, and protect the rights of posterity. Errant governments can wage unnecessary wars, squander the national treasure and reputation, make disastrous environmental choices, and deregulate banks and financial institutions, with catastrophic results. *In other words, we will rise or fall by what governments do or fail to do. The long emergency ahead will be the ultimate challenge to our political creativity, acumen, skill, wisdom and foresight.**

While all of the aforementioned issues have private-sector implications, consequences, and connections, they are for the most part public-sector issues, concerns, and problems, and will therefore have to be dealt with primarily in the public realm and by public sector institutions. Even stimulating the Canadian economy and dealing successfully with Canadian corporations and financial institutions has become a major public-sector responsibility if the country's corporations and companies are to act in the best interests of Canada, Canadians, and Canadian culture and not their own best interests or the best interests of their shareholders and chief

---

* David Orr, *Down to the Wire: Confronting Climate Collapse* (New York: Oxford University Press, 2009), pp. 7–8 (italics mine).

executive officers. This is most apparent in terms of corporate responsibilities with respect to the environment and many social issues, but it is also apparent in other areas, such as fraudulent accounting practices, exorbitant payouts to senior executives, corporate bailouts and subsidies, the ability of corporations to challenge governments in investment courts if they interfere with their ability to make profits, and so forth. All these matters, and many others, require powerful governmental and public sector actions and initiatives if they are to be dealt with effectively.

After more than two centuries of preoccupation with the private sector and private sector organizations, the pendulum has begun to swing in the opposite direction—and swing rapidly. Without doubt, Canada's public sector will have to play a direct, proactive, and forceful role if these and other issues, concerns, and problems are to be overcome in the years and decades ahead.

This is an area where Canada and Canada's public sector could—and indeed should—play an exemplary role in the world of the future. People and countries in all parts of the world are desperately in need of a country in general—and governments, educational institutions, and civil society organizations in particular—capable of restoring people's confidence in the public sector and standing up to corporations, wealthy elites, and powerful establishments where this is necessary or required.

If Canada can achieve this in the remaining decades of the twenty-first century, it will fill the exemplary role required not just in Canada but throughout the world. For just as Canadian athletes reached the point where they realized that they had to "own the podium" if they were to be successful in their athletic endeavours, so governments, educational institutions, civil society organizations, and other public sector agencies and institutions will have to "act in the public interest" if real progress is to be made in this area. This is why a new political and public reality is required to make this a practical and concrete reality and not just a theoretical and abstract ideal.

It is not the intention here to downplay the importance of Canada's private sector. It has an essential role to play and a great deal to contribute to the development of Canada and Canadian culture in a whole series of deep, dynamic, and diverse ways in the future. This should never change. But it *is* the intention to ensure that the private sector and private-sector organizations do not dominate the public sector and public sector institutions, and that public-sector issues and concerns take precedence over private-sector issues and concerns. This is because the public sector and its many diverse institutions are more concerned with advancing the interests of people and environmental well-being than producing profits and promoting excessive amounts of consumerism, commercialism, and materialism.

Clearly a breakthrough is needed in this area and Canada is one of the very few countries in the world—*if not the only country*—that is capable of making it. If Canada and Canadians can achieve a real breakthrough in this area, this will not only benefit this country and its citizenry, but also people and countries in other parts of the world and the world as a whole. With governments in general and the federal government in particular taking the lead and providing the impetus required to set this process in motion and steer it in the right direction in concrete and practical terms, we are now in a perfect position to turn our attention to the next step in this process. While this breakthrough is necessary at all levels, it is especially necessary at the municipal or local level since this is the level that most directly affects people's everyday lives.

CHAPTER EIGHT

Livable Neighbourhoods, Towns, and Cities

C anada's towns, cities, and neighbourhoods are fascinating
places. Ranging in size and character all the way from the Atlantic in the east to the Pacific in the west and the Arctic in the
north, they are filled with a vast panorama of individuals, institutions,
facilities, programs, activities, and delights.

Everything is there in one form or another: schools, hospitals, banks,
insurance companies, homes, offices, gardens, religious institutions,
corporations, governments, small businesses, recreational endeavours, art
galleries, museums, concert halls, parks, restaurants, and most of all,
people.

Also there, although far more difficult to detect, are the cultures of
these towns, cities, and neighbourhoods. These cultures result from the
fact that past and present generations of Canadians have combined all the
various activities in which they have been and are engaged—economic,
social, political, educational, artistic, athletic, technological, environmental, and so forth—to form wholes that are greater than the parts and the
sum of the parts. This is what gives these cultures their distinctiveness and
identity, since no two are the same.

Unfortunately, it is not possible to see these cultures as wholes because
they are composed of far too many parts, and the ordering process and
organizational principles used to combine all the parts together to form
dynamic and organic wholes are equally difficult to discern. What one can
see, however, are some of the most important symbolic parts that constitute these cultures. The most obvious example of this in the Canadian case
is hockey. Not only does hockey exist in physical and material form in
every town, city, and neighbourhood across the country, but also it plays a
pivotal role in shaping the character and identity of the cultures of these

places. This makes it possible get a *sense* or *feel* for what these cultures are like in the holistic sense, through one of their most distinctive and representative parts.

For many Canadians, hockey is, was, and always will be their game and their passion. We are constantly reminded of this during the myriad radio and television broadcasts of hockey games in Canada, as well as Rogers' Hometown Hockey project, Scotiabank's Community Hockey Sponsorship Program and Heroes of Hockey Day, Kraft Hockeyville, books like Ken Dryden and Roy McGregor's *Home Game: Hockey and Life in Canada*, and numerous other publications and events. This is reinforced by the fact that many Canadians played hockey at a local rink or ball hockey on the street. If they were good enough, they might also have played for a junior or senior team, and, if they were exceptionally talented and worked incredibly hard, possibly even an NHL team. More likely, however, they coached a hockey team or some other sports team where they grew up or live today. There are even those who continue to play hockey well into their seventies and possibly even their eighties.

There is much to be learned from the example of hockey that is relevant to getting a sense or feel for what the cultures of the country's towns, cities, and neighbourhoods are like in the all-encompassing sense. And it is not only hockey or some other athletic activity such as curling or baseball that provides this. The country's artists, scholars, and other types of creative people play a key role here as well, since they are skilled at selecting specific parts of these cultures that are symbolic of the whole and therefore "stand for the whole" in the fundamental sense discussed earlier. This makes it possible for them to communicate a great deal of insight into what local and municipal cultures are like as wholes or overall ways of life through exposure to some of their most salient and revealing parts, much as Harold Innis did when he selected fish and fur as the focus for his own valuable insights into the nature of the Canadian economy during a very distinct period in the country's development.

Two artists who have been particularly effective at giving Canadians a sense or feel for what the cultures of the country's towns, cities, and neighbourhoods are like in the all-inclusive sense are Mordecai Richler and Alice Munro. Richler did so by writing about growing up in a specific neighbourhood of Montreal around St. Urbain Street, which he was able to contrast with other neighbourhoods such as Westmount and Outremont, in his popular book *The Apprenticeship of Duddy Kravitz* (later made into a movie). Alice Munro did so by writing in her book *Lives of Girls and*

Women about growing up in and near a small, mythical town called Jubilee, located somewhere in Huron County in southwestern Ontario. (Jubilee is believed to have been inspired by the town of Wingham, where Munro herself grew up.) What emerges from both books as the stories unfold is a sense or feeling for what the cultures of these places were like as wholes at a very specific time through exposure to some of their most symbolic and representative parts.

What is true for Richler and Munro and their two books is also true for many other Canadian authors and their books, as well as for other types of artists and scholars and their works. This is what makes the writings of creative people like the two aforementioned literary giants and many others so valuable. The country's libraries and bookstores, as well as millions of Canadian homes, are filled with literary masterpieces and materials of many different kinds that shed a great deal of light on the cultures of Canada's neighbourhoods, towns, and cities.

And this is not all. Often the smaller the place, the more is revealed about its culture and its character. Stephen Leacock illustrated this fact in his book *Sunshine Sketches of a Little Town*. Many believe the town Leacock was writing about was Orillia, where he had grown up and spent most of his youth, although this was cleverly disguised in the book. Nevertheless, it irked many people in Orillia who were identified as characters in the book, especially when Leacock depicted them in a satirical way.

What does all this have to do with Canada in the twenty-first century? Actually, a great deal. There is no better place to start the exemplary process advocated earlier—as well as to illustrate how essential it is to take a cultural and chronological approach to all this—than with Canada's towns, cities, and neighbourhoods. Not only are cultures easier to understand, experience, and identify with at the local as opposed to the national level, but the country's towns and cities are growing rapidly in size and stature and thus playing a stronger and more powerful role in Canadian development. If Canada's towns, cities, and neighbourhoods lack the resources, infrastructure, and capabilities required to be vital, viable, dynamic, livable wholes comprised of many interrelated parts, no developments at other levels will make up the difference. This is probably why two of Canada's most respected and distinguished authors, Northrop Frye and Jane Jacobs, talked at length about the importance of Canada's neighbourhoods, towns, and cities—in the case of Jacobs, especially neighbourhoods—in the development of Canada and its culture.

There is another compelling reason for commencing this exemplary process at the local or municipal level. If Canadians can get the cultural development of the country's towns, cities, and neighbourhoods right during the remaining decades of the twenty-first century, they will likely get most other things right as well, not only at this level but also at the provincial, territorial, regional, national, and international levels. This is because the country's towns, cities, and neighbourhoods have a great deal to teach us about what is most essential and worthwhile in life, how life and living can be addressed most effectively, what being a responsible citizen of Canada actually means, and what changes are required in lifestyles, attitudes, behaviour, and ways of life.

Regardless of where they eventually end up, what they work at, or how they live their lives, the rootedness, connectedness, and experiences young people are exposed to in their families, homes, schools, churches, synagogues, mosques, gymnasiums, rinks, soccer fields, and so forth play an indispensable role in making them who they are as adults. These places are where friendships are formed, associations are made, and a strong sense of identity, belonging, citizenship, and pride of place is fashioned and cultivated. It is also where people learn a great deal about the specific cultures they are immersed in and the many different activities, events, organizations, and so forth that constitute these cultures.

These experiences are often replayed much later in life at the thousands of reunions that take place across the country every year. There isn't a day goes by that reunions of one sort or another don't take place in neighbourhoods, towns, and cities all across Canada for sports teams, schools, choirs and bands, ethnic, religious, spiritual, and charitable organizations, environmental groups, and virtually everything else. They provide opportunities for Canadians who shared many bonds and connections in the past to reminisce about old times, exchange information on what friends and colleagues are doing today, trade email addresses, telephone numbers, and business cards, and make plans for the future.

As every Canadian knows, friendships and associations formed in childhood and youth often last for decades and even a lifetime. These relationships can—and often do—play a crucial role in finding jobs and securing contracts later in life, learning about important investment, travel, recreational, and culinary opportunities, meeting spouses, and developing networks and support systems of one type or another.

As a result of these and other activities, Canada's towns, cities, and neighbourhoods are ideal places to learn about the rights and responsibilities of citizenship, thereby addressing one of the most important objectives for Canada's governments and its educational system and institutions. Giving back is a fundamental aspect of the responsibilities of a citizen, although doing so will probably occur in a different place than where most Canadians grew up because of today's high rate of mobility and occupational turnover. Nevertheless, giving back is critical, regardless of where Canadians live and work, especially if the country is to thrive and prosper. There are certain responsibilities associated with being a Canadian citizen, such as improving the quality of life and well-being for future generations, participating in a variety of worthwhile social events and humanitarian causes, beautifying homes, gardens, and neighbourhoods through landscaping, public art, and murals, making improvements in specific aspects of local life, and so forth. Having experienced and benefited from such experiences while growing up, many Canadians find themselves in a position where they are able to provide similar opportunities for their children, grandchildren, relatives, friends, young people, and those who are less fortunate than themselves.

Margaret Thatcher, former prime minister of the United Kingdom, once said that there is no such thing as community, only collectivities of individuals. How wrong she was! Like culture and cultures, community and communities reside at the heart and soul of what is most important and worthwhile in life. This fact has become steadily more apparent, now that more than fifty percent of the world's population lives in urban centres of various shapes and sizes. In Canada, more than half of the country's population lives in four huge, rapidly expanding urban centres— the Montreal area, the Greater Toronto-Golden Horseshoe area, Calgary-Edmonton, and Vancouver. Many more Canadians live in smaller but equally important urban areas such as Winnipeg, Halifax, Moncton, Regina, Saint John's, Ottawa, and others. Moreover, all predictions indicate that the proportion of Canadians living in urban areas will continue to grow.

This means that future generations of Canadians will have to develop the rootedness, grounding, values, and sense of identity needed to be responsible citizens in these urban settings. It also means that the large majority of Canadians will be looking to the country's neighbourhoods, towns, and cities to solve their economic, social, environmental, educational, recreational, and technological problems, and to address their individual and collective needs. They will expect these places to provide fulfilling jobs, a decent standard of living, an excellent quality of life, more

113

meaningful career opportunities, a great deal more environmental sustainability, affordable housing, and greater safety and security. If Canada's urban centres are not able to provide the infrastructure and resources required for the country's citizens to live happy, healthy, safe, and creative lives in the years and decades ahead, developments at other levels will not close the gap.

And this raises a very interesting question. What is it that makes Canada's neighbourhoods, towns, and cities *"livable?"* Why is living and working in one Canadian neighbourhood, town, or city exciting and exhilarating whereas living and working in another is difficult and demanding?

Jane Jacobs addressed questions like this as one of Canada's and the world's foremost authorities on urban development. What she emphasized above all else was the need for a *balanced, diversified,* and *integrated* array of social, economic, artistic, recreational, spiritual, educational, environmental, culinary, and other opportunities and amenities, especially at the neighbourhood level. Possessing these resources close to home and within easy walking distance helps to make urban life much more livable, especially when these resources are fully integrated into other aspects of local life.

Many factors contribute to this. One is stimulating jobs and job prospects. Another is superb social programs and educational institutions. Yet another is outstanding libraries, hospitals, and health care facilities and services. And still others are effective transportation and communications systems, numerous pedestrian walkways, suitable land-use and life-work arrangements, a variety of housing styles and types, memorable public squares and spaces, beautiful buildings, excellent restaurants, and exquisite parks and gardens. Think, for example, about what Butchart Gardens, Stanley Park, Point Pleasant Park, and the Royal Botanical Gardens mean to Victoria, Vancouver, Halifax, and Hamilton-Burlington respectively. To this should be added a variety of athletic, commercial, and shopping possibilities, historic buildings and monuments, favourite haunts and hideaways, the availability of farmers' markets like those in Kitchener-Waterloo, Ottawa, and Fredericton, stimulating ambiance, and captivating ways to idle away the day. All these factors, and others, contribute to livable urban environments in Canada, both now and in the future.

This is an area where Canada and Canadians are already demonstrating a great deal of international leadership and doing a significant amount of pioneering and exemplary work. The creation and development of the

Creative City Network of Canada in Vancouver in 1997 paved the way for much of this. For almost twenty years now, this organization has been promoting the need to invest more heavily in the creative potential of Canadians and the development of cultures at the municipal level, as well as conducting numerous workshops and summits across the country to bring people, institutions, and urban experts together to understand how this can be achieved in fact. As a result, this remarkable organization is well-known across the country and around the world for "kick-starting" the movement and commitment to "creative cities." It is also being actively embraced in other parts of the world that are anxious to capitalize on its expertise and emulate its achievements in this area.

The same holds true for Richard Florida and his pioneering work on urban development. Interestingly, Florida came to Canada from the United States to work at the Martin Prosperity Institute at the University of Toronto. He is well known throughout the world for his valuable research and writing on "the creative class" and the dynamic role it plays in urban development. His books and research into this matter in general—and his popular book *The Rise of the Creative Class: How It's Transforming Work, Leisure, Community and Everyday Life* in particular—document in detail how creative people in many towns and cities across the country and around the world—artists, designers, activists, inventors, animators, advertisers, architects, doctors, lawyers, town planners, and so forth—are providing the impetus that is required to broaden and deepen developments in all areas of urban life. This is helping to create the wealth, well-being, and sense of belonging, identity, and accomplishment that are required to make towns and cities livable, dynamic, and unique rather than lethargic, static, and dull.

The arts have a crucial role to play as well. For one thing, they bring an enormous amount of joy and happiness into the lives of millions of town and city dwellers across the country and throughout the world by conveying "the highest quality to your moments as they pass," as Walter Pater so astutely expressed it. Many Canadians will no longer locate in urban settings that lack a diversity of artistic undertakings and institutions, especially art galleries, museums, theatre and dance companies, symphony orchestras, art centres, festivals, concerts, plays, and so forth.

The arts also contribute a great deal to the social cohesion and well-being of Canada's urban environments. They do so through their ability to engage large numbers of people in the artistic process as audience members and active participants. They also contribute significantly to the economies of these places. This occurs through their ability to generate billions of dollars of investment and expenditure on hotels, restaurants, capital facilities, equipment, ticket sales, clothing, transportation, tourism, and the like. They also attract business, industry, and skilled workers. Like citizens, many corporations will not locate in towns and cities that are devoid of stimulating artistic endeavours and aesthetic experiences.

The arts also make indispensable contributions to the attractiveness of the country's neighbourhoods, towns, and cities, both at present and hopefully to an even greater degree in the future. They do so through a variety of activities and programs, not just the activities and programs of large, professional performing and exhibiting arts organizations. Community arts centres and arts councils, neighbourhood arts festivals, murals on the sides of buildings, buskers on city streets, and the architectural, environmental, horticultural, material, and culinary arts add richness, vitality, originality, diversity, and distinctiveness to Canada's urban landscapes. So do the artistic works of children and young people. Is there anything more delightful than a children's art exhibition at the local arena, a high school play, a youth choir singing at the civic centre, or an annual music night?

To this must be added the contribution the arts make to safety, security, harmony, and cross-cultural fertilization, understanding, interaction, and exchange. The arts bring people, ethnic groups, and cultures together in humane and peaceful rather than violent and inhumane ways. This will be increasingly important for Canada and the world in the years and decades ahead as racial, ethnic, and religious strife, tensions, differences, and conflicts escalate and populations become more unstable, diverse, and heterogeneous in character.

While the arts are capable of making substantial contributions in all these areas, their contributions do not end here. Recent research is revealing that the arts contribute to the development, livability, and authenticity of Canada's towns, cities, and neighbourhoods in other significant ways.

One of these ways is through the energy, vitality, and creativity they inject into all aspects of local life. By creating many of the concepts, contents, contexts, styles, methods, and techniques that are required to initiate and facilitate change and stimulate creative place-making and place-keeping, artists and arts organizations pave the way for many other developments. It is not surprising in this regard that urban planners and policy-makers are increasingly focused on the role that "the creative industries" play in urban development—creative industries such as the arts, social media, advertising, and micro-enterprises that produce "clustering effects" and "convergent possibilities" that link various segments and sectors of communities, towns, and cities together.

Equally important are the contributions the arts make to revitalization, revival, renewal, transformation, and change. This has been demonstrated time and again in cities across the country in recent years—cities as geographically separated as Vancouver, Calgary, Winnipeg, Toronto, Montreal, Moncton, Halifax, and St. John's—where dynamic arts organizations and stimulating cultural hubs, corridors, and districts are injecting new life into areas of these cities after decades of disinterest or neglect. These organizations, corridors, hubs, and districts involve large concentrations and constellations of artistic, athletic, media, heritage, entertainment, commercial and gastronomic resources located in key areas in the downtown core or surrounding suburbs. Inspired by artists, arts administrators, town planners, politicians, developers, and citizens, they are doing a great deal to rejuvenate many Canadian towns and cities.

Consistent with the experience of countless towns and cities across the country and elsewhere in the world, as well as much of the contemporary evidence, there is an interactive, reinforcing, and reciprocal—rather than unilateral and parasitical—relationship between the arts, neighbourhoods, towns, and cities. The arts energize and enrich Canada's urban centres. In return, these places broaden, deepen, and intensify developments in the arts. All individuals and institutions benefit from this process and the profuse economic, commercial, financial, and non-financial rewards that are derived from this.

Recognition of this fact should open the doors to a dramatic increase in funding for the arts at the municipal level. This funding should come from all levels of governments—federal, provincial, territorial, regional, and municipal—as well as corporations, foundations, and private donors. While funding from capital budgets, partnership programs, and special reserves is important, funding should come principally from annual appropriations and general revenues. *And it should be for operating as well as capital purposes.* Funding that produces physical facilities but does not provide for high-quality programs will not suffice.

There is a great need for some strategic rethinking here. Rather than viewing funding for the arts as an *expenditure* that must be tolerated, it should be viewed as an *investment* that must be embraced. It is an investment capable of producing multiple, cumulative, and long-term benefits, as well as eliciting and activating other possibilities. Funding that generates clustering and integrative effects and activates other opportunities—such as funding for renewal and revitalization, transformation and change, creation of cultural hubs, cores, and corridors, facilitation of experimental and experiential works, training of skilled workers, and so forth—plays a pivotal role in municipal development and decision-making and is imperative if the objective is to inject new life and vitality into Canada's neighbourhoods, towns and cities and make them more viable, exciting, and dynamic in the future.

Arts animators, administrators, entrepreneurs, and activists capable of creating new programs and projects, initiating change, and engaging large numbers of people in the artistic process have a particularly important role to play here. There is simply no substitute for well-trained and highly creative people who are skilled at getting people involved in a variety of artistic and cultural activities and stimulating other possibilities. As Charles Landry, one of the world's leading authorities on the development of the arts and creative cities, states, "wealth in cities is created less by what we produce and more by how we use our brains and add value through knowledge and imagination. Cities now have one crucial resource—their people. Human cleverness, ingenuity, and creativity are replacing location, natural resources, and market access as urban assets. We need to provide the conditions to unleash this."

Nothing does this better than arts education. Education in this area, especially when it involves outstanding instruction by skilled teachers and is combined with involvement by a variety of community-based organizations and individual artists, provides the foundation for other developments. When the arts are decimated by funding cuts—much as they have been in many educational institutions across the country in recent years— the result is the loss of important programs and courses as well as apathy and neglect. This prevents the arts from making their full contribution to the development of healthy, vigorous, sustainable, and civilized towns and cities.

Not only do music, drama, dance, the visual arts, and other art forms unlock the ingenuity inherent in Canadians at all ages and stages in life, but they also help to ensure that they engage in positive and constructive rather than negative and destructive forms of behaviour. They also provide training opportunities for future generations of artists, as well as educating discerning and discriminating audiences. Without a comprehensive and compelling education in the arts, judiciously designed to produce concrete outcomes and practical results, it will not be possible for future generations of Canadians to live decent, humane, and fulfilling lives.

Toronto provides an excellent example of the type of artistic renaissance and cultural transformation that is needed and possible in many parts of Canada at the municipal level. This artistic renaissance and cultural transformation is being driven by a broad array of artists and arts organizations and is stimulating a great deal of commercial, industrial, residential, tourist, and entrepreneurial activity. Included in this renaissance and transformation are recent renovations of the Art Gallery of Ontario, the Royal Ontario Museum, and the Ontario College of Art and Design; creation of the Distillery District and Liberty Village in former (and long neglected) industrial areas; creation of a "cultural corridor" along Bloor Street that is linking the Royal Ontario Museum, the Bata Shoe Museum, the Gardiner Museum, the University of Toronto, the Royal Conservatory of Music, Koerner Hall, and other institutions together; and captivating developments in and around Ryerson University that include the remarkable make-over of Maple Leaf Gardens and a host of other innovative accomplishments in the Yonge and Dundas area. These developments are producing myriad social, commercial, educational, and aesthetic benefits for residents and visitors alike.

Artscape is playing a very active and valuable role in this process. This is yet another Canadian organization that is rapidly becoming well-known internationally for its pioneering work in urban development, renewal, revitalization, and reform. This is especially true with respect to the way it is bringing artists and other creative people together with developers, planners, and citizens to create spaces and places that engage citizens fully and actively in a planning and development process designed to meet the needs and interests of people and not just corporations and developers in both capital and operating terms. Commencing with its inventive Wychwood Barns project, Artscape has been successful in creating or contributing to the development of a number of key cultural hubs and corridors in different parts of Toronto. Included are the West Queen West area around Parkdale and Crawford Street, the resurgence and revitalization of Regent Park, and, more recently, the creation of a major cultural hub in the Junction and Weston region that is building bridges between many artistic, social, industrial, developers,' and citizens' coalitions and constituencies.

These developments are being reinforced by the Daniels Corporation, which has been active in Toronto for many years in creating and building condominiums intimately connected with the arts and culture, such as the redevelopment of Regent Park in conjunction with Toronto Community Housing. One of its most recent projects is the City of the Arts located in the Toronto Waterfront area at the foot of Jarvis Street and Queens Quay. It is providing its Lighthouse Tower and other residents with a convenient "connectivity package" that includes a variety of benefits provided by Artscape, the Toronto International Film Festival, and North by North West, such as passes to art galleries, workshops, and presentations by artists, film screenings, exclusive productions, and opening night celebrations. This is helping to make condominium life more enjoyable than it was in the past.

These and other developments have put Toronto on the international map as one of the most stimulating, interesting, and enjoyable places in the world in which to live and work. Over the last several decades and particularly during the last few years, Toronto has been recognized as one of the most livable cities in the world—if not *the* most livable—by the United Nations, The Economist Intelligence Unit, *Metropolis* magazine, Mercer's Quality of Life Ranking, and others. Most rankings are based on a variety of criteria, such as safety, security, education, heath care, environment, recreation, political stability, walkability, preservation of heritage sites, and others.

Toronto was also ranked "the best city in the world for youth" in a survey commissioned by the New York-based Citi Foundation. This survey delved deeply into employment and growth statistics in addition to the strength of government programs, educational institutions, and entrepreneurial opportunities for people in the 18-to-25 age range. It revealed that Toronto was the most effective city in the world in terms of providing jobs, business opportunities, and entrepreneurial possibilities for young people. This is one of the most pressing requirements in Canada and the world today because of the high rate of occupational turnover, unemployment, underemployment, and precarious employment among youth.

Developments similar to those in Toronto are taking place in other Canadian cities such as Montreal, Vancouver, and Calgary that also rank high on international rankings and ratings. Montreal, for instance, is quickly acquiring a reputation as one of the most attractive and enjoyable cities in the world in which to live and work (as well as visit), due primarily to the development of the Quartier des Spectacles, which includes La Vitrine, Place des Arts, the Musé d'Art contemporaine de Montréal, as well as equally important developments in Old Montreal like the well-known

Notre Dame Basilica, Montreal Museum of Archaeology and History, Centre d'histoire de Montréal, Arsenal Contemporary Arts, and, more recently, the Cité Mémoire, which enables residents and tourists alike to journey through time by means of the project's after-dark tableaux. This complements such cherished institutions and landmarks in this city as the McCord Museum, the Canadian Centre for Architecture, Sainte Catherine Street, Galeria MX, and the Montreal Arts Council, which is one of the oldest and most successful and active arts councils in Canada and the world.

In recent years, this has been enhanced by the development of a great deal of street art and murals, thereby contributing to the aesthetic appeal and character of Montreal. Particularly important in this regard are developments by such organizations as Être Avec Toi (Ê.A.T), which is composed largely of a "who's who" of famous graffiti and street artists from Montreal and other parts of the world, as well as MASSIVart Mural Festival, which is concerned largely with painting murals on the sides of buildings and other significant structures. Due to developments like this, Montreal was the first Canadian city to be added to Google's street art gallery with more than 150 major murals in place, thereby contributing to Montreal's rapidly evolving reputation as an "artistic city" of major importance and considerable stature in the world.

Given the contributions the arts and culture make to the development of neighbourhoods, towns, and cities in all parts of the country—many of which strike at the heart and soul of what urban life, living, and development are all about, both at present and even more so in the future—the role of the arts and culture in Canada's municipal development should be seen in a new light. Rather than being viewed as "the icing on the cake" and "an afterthought," as has all too often been the case, the arts and culture should be viewed as the *centrepiece* and *spearhead* needed to propel Canada's neighbourhoods, towns, and cities to lofty heights.

This is especially true for culture. Seeing and treating culture in this way is consistent with conclusions arrived at recently by a number of international organizations and agencies, such as Agenda 21 and the Global Task Force on Local and Regional Governments. This is what the Task Force had to say about culture in its 2014 report: "*Culture will be key to the success of sustainable development policies, as driver and enabler of development and people-centered societies. A holistic and integrated approach to development needs to take creativity, heritage, knowledge, and diversity into account. Poverty is not just a question of material con-*

ditions and income, but also the lack of capabilities and opportunities in cultural terms."

These sentiments were reinforced by three internationally known and distinguished experts on culture and sustainable urban development—Nancy Duxbury, Jyoti Hosagrahar, and Jordi Pascual—in a 2016 paper, "Why Must Culture Be at the Heart of Sustainable Urban Development?" Here is what these authors had to say about this matter: "In the context of defining a new people-centred and planet-sensitive sustainable development agenda, cities are transformative platforms. To create a new culturally sensitive urban development model, the role of cultural policies and values in sustainable development must now be recognized, supported, and integrated into planning and policy in a systematic and comprehensive way."

The authors went on to single out local cultures for special treatment and attention in a companion piece entitled "How Local Cultures Contribute to the Sustainable Development of Cities." Their thoughts on this matter resonate strongly with the point made earlier that understanding and developing local cultures is the key to urban development in the future: "Local cultures encompass the traditional, long-standing, and evolving cultures of a territory as well as the cultures of new arrivals to the area—and the evolutionary and hybrid transformations that evolve from living and creating within culturally diverse contexts. Local cultural vitality and its dynamic transmission are desirable ends in themselves." The authors go on to say, "We all need to learn about the past of our city, so that we can 'own' it and propel this identity and local knowledge into the future. Local cultures allow citizens to gain ownership of the city, and to meet and learn from one another—in short, culture is a means through which citizens feel they belong to their city."

It follows that if Canada's neighbourhoods, towns, and cities are to be exciting places in which to live, work, and enjoy life to the fullest extent in the future, it will be necessary to broaden, deepen, and intensify municipal cultural development well beyond its present level.

Many resources will have to be created and cultivated to make this a reality. These resources have to do with coming to grips with environmental deterioration, poverty, homelessness, unemployment, lack of suitable and affordable housing, the aging population, escalating religious and ethnic tensions and divides, racial prejudice, complex transportation and communications problems, insufficient and crumbling infrastructure, and so forth.

These resources are urgently needed to address environmental problems, upgrade and expand transportation and communications systems, eradicate poverty and homelessness, enhance ethnic, racial, and religious tolerance, and improve the welfare and well-being of Canadian citizens. They are also required to ensure greater emergency preparedness and training on the part of police forces, hospitals, governments, schools, and voluntary organizations, as well as to create many more facilities, programs, and cures for people suffering from debilitating diseases and illnesses, to integrate immigrants, refugees, and newcomers more fully into Canadian society and culture, and to make life and living enjoyable for all people. If children, young people, adults, and seniors do not feel safe in their homes, communities, streets, subways, buses, and neighbourhoods—and if they do not feel secure in the places where they live, work, worship, and study—no amount of resources deployed in other areas or at other levels will make up the difference.

Some fundamental changes will be required in the way Canada's towns and cities are financed and administered in the future if these and other requirements are to be met. Municipal governments currently lack the constitutional authority, financial resources, taxation powers, and institutional mechanisms that are needed. There is an old adage in Canada that the federal government has the money, the provincial governments have the power, and the municipal governments have the problems. There is a great deal of truth to this. While battles are constantly being waged between the federal and provincial governments over money and power, municipal governments are compelled to struggle with a whole host of difficult problems. However, as more Canadians look to municipal governments to solve their problems and when federal and provincial governments expect municipal governments to deal with a rapidly expanding array of complex environmental, social, safety, security, health, and transportation issues, municipal governments find themselves in an awkward and challenging position. With limited ability to raise revenues and more demands and responsibilities being placed on them, municipal governments face the worst of all possible worlds. This problem can be traced back to the British North America Act of 1867, which made municipalities the responsibility of the provinces and territories and gave them few powers of their own. While this worked well enough when the country was primarily rural and agrarian in nature, it is no longer desirable or effective now that three-quarters of the Canadian population is living in towns and cities.

This is why there have been strong and vocal demands in recent years for a "new deal for cities" and a very different system of municipal financing, administration, and development in the future. These demands are being voiced by an expanding number of municipal planners, policy-makers, civic servants, and local politicians, as well as by newspapers, community groups, and some corporate leaders. They are also being voiced in numerous studies and reports, such as those conducted by the Conference Board of Canada, the Urban Development Institute, the Canadian Urban Institute, the Federation of Canadian Municipalities, and others. The consensus in these studies, reports, and organizations is clear and unequivocal. Without a new system for dealing with municipal finance, governance, and management, Canada will pay a steep price. As Anne Golden, former head of the Conference Board of Canada, once said, "The plight of cities is not simply a problem for urban dwellers. How effectively Canadian cities work determines the overall success of Canada."

The short-term solution to this problem is to increase municipal revenues. This can be done in a number of ways. The most obvious way is through increased property taxes, especially as property values have risen much more rapidly than the amount collected in property taxes in recent years. Other ways to increase municipal revenues include increased user fees on publicly owned and operated buildings, programs, and services such as waste collection, treatment, and disposal; the creation of more lotteries and similar fund-raising schemes; and the selling off of municipal assets and properties. Still other ways include increased taxes on corporations and developers, as well as larger transfers of funds from the other levels of government.

Of these alternatives, many citizens and municipal politicians prefer increased transfers from other levels of government. There is a reason for this. Many Canadians and municipal politicians feel that property taxes are already too high—although this will have to be revisited in the future if present trends concerning the value of people's properties continue—and municipal governments depend too heavily on this source, since more than half of their revenue comes from taxes on property. As well, there are limits to how much revenue can be generated through user fees, licensing fees, lotteries, and so on. In addition, many Canadians are reluctant to see municipalities rely more heavily on raising taxes on corporations and developers because they think this would put corporations and developers in an even stronger position to influence municipal policies.

This explains why more funding from the other levels of government is the most attractive alternative, especially in the short term. It is also the case that the federal and provincial governments have in recent years downloaded numerous programs and responsibilities to municipal governments and therefore should be paying a much greater share of the cost. There are many examples of such downloading. Over the last few decades, the federal government has retreated from the leadership role it once played in providing funding for social housing, largely as a result of attempts to rein in budgetary deficits. It also placed eligibility restrictions on Employment Insurance and eliminated the Canada Assistance Plan, the only national anti-poverty program that was cost-shared with the provincial, territorial, and municipal governments. The provincial governments have likewise disengaged from many social responsibilities and downloaded programs to the municipalities with little or no compensation in return. This has caused a "social deficit" and "infrastructure gap" that is a sore point among most municipal leaders and governments today.

Another possibility is for municipal governments to sign more partnership and cost-sharing arrangements with other levels of government. There have been a number of examples of such agreements, including the Urban Development Agreement that was signed between the city of Vancouver, the province of British Columbia, and the federal government to cover various economic, social, and community development costs in Vancouver, as well as the Winnipeg Development Agreement between the city of Winnipeg, the province of Manitoba, and the federal government to promote downtown revitalization and create an employment equity program that focused on jobs and the training of Indigenous groups, individuals with disabilities, visible minorities, and women.

As these possibilities suggest, it is not difficult to visualize new partnership and cost-sharing agreements that could be worked out to advantage between the federal, provincial, territorial, and municipal governments to address a panorama of possibilities, concerns, and needs at the municipal level. Another viable possibility would be for the other two levels of governments to provide municipalities with GST rebates for such programs as green infrastructure projects, water and sewage treatment, renewable energy generation and energy control systems, public transit, and the development of more energy-efficient homes, factories, buildings, and offices.

As valuable as these solutions may be in the short term, there is no substitute for putting municipal governments on a much firmer long-term financial foundation. If Canadian municipalities are to remain competitive with their counterparts elsewhere in the world, they need to be able to access a much larger share of the public financial pie in the future. This should come from legislative changes that make it possible, for instance, for municipal governments to share fuel, gasoline, and sales taxes, as well as to impose taxes of their own on the sale of alcohol and tobacco as well as on institutions such as hotels, restaurants, and retail establishments that benefit immensely from municipal services but pay little of the cost of providing these developments and services. The experience with similar arrangements in the United States and many European countries indicates that when municipal governments possess the authority to impose taxes like these and actually do so in fact, the entire community benefits from the impetus this provides to commercial, industrial, and tourist development and the strengthening of local economies and cultures.

While increasing the tax-levying capacity of municipal governments is a necessary step in the right direction, ultimately it may be necessary to change the legislative arrangements that govern the relationship of the country's federal, provincial, territorial, and municipal governments. A good example of this was the willingness of the Ontario government in recent years to empower cities to require builders to include affordable housing in all new residential developments. This "inclusionary zoning capacity," as it was called, required developers to set aside a certain percentage of all new units for low- and moderate-income households as part of the affordable housing strategy devised by the provincial government.

What is also required is a much more inclusive and cooperative approach to municipal planning, policy, and decision-making in the future. In the past, this approach has often been partial, partisan, piecemeal, and exclusive, rather than systematic, equitable, comprehensive, and sustainable. This must change. If Canada's neighbourhoods, towns, and cities are to prosper and be livable in the decades ahead, the emphasis will have to be on creating urban centres that possess a rich and diverse array of cultural resources and opportunities that are fully integrated into Canadian culture and accessible to all Canadians.

What we are talking about here is "the new urbanism" and "smart growth." This is based on taking a cultural and holistic approach—rather than a partial and specialized approach—to municipal planning, policy, and decision-making. The emphasis should be on building neighbourhoods, towns, and cities that are inclusive and creative rather than segregated, segmented, and imitative. This means creating urban spaces capable of conserving and not only consuming resources, protecting the natural environment and local habitats rather than destroying them, and refreshing and revitalizing people at every opportunity. This can only be achieved by focusing on the entire "culturescapes"* of the country's neighbourhoods, towns, and cities and consequently the collective statements they make to themselves and the rest of the world.

Seen from this perspective, Canada's urban environments really are cultures composed of many interrelated and diverse parts—economic, social, environmental, recreational, technological, scientific, educational, artistic, spiritual, and the like. Not only do these parts vary significantly from one another in many ways, but also they vary significantly in the way they are combined together to form wholes and overall ways of life. To be effective, all the many different parts must function effectively and be fully integrated into the whole, and harmonious relationships must be established between and among these parts. This is, in the final analysis, the essence of "livability," today and even more so in the future. Livability encompasses the individual and collective experiences, feelings, and fulfillment that result when people live together, share the same space together, inspire each other, and imprint their needs, interests, ideas, and actions on a very specific piece of the world's geography.

It follows from this that culture and cultures enter into municipal development and decision-making in a very different way than all other activities. Whereas all other activities are parts of the whole—notes in the melody, so to speak—culture and cultures are the cement that binds all the various parts together to form wholes that are greater than the parts and the sum of the parts. This is what makes it possible to talk about the cultures of Canada's towns and cities and mean something profound, powerful, and practical by this. It is also what makes culture *the* most important factor in municipal development and decision-making. It is culture in general—and cultural cohesion, bonding, and creativity in particular—that ensure that Canada's urban environments are stimulating and coherent wholes, rather than merely random, disconnected, and unrelated parts.

Every individual and institution in Canada has a valuable role to play in this process. This includes teachers, social workers, athletes, artists, charitable organizations, environmental agencies, and educational institutions

---

* The concept of culturescapes is discussed in detail in my book *The Age of Culture* (Rock's Mills Press, 2014).

as well as lawyers, politicians, business executives, corporations, and governments. It is the sum total of all individuals and institutions in Canada—and especially their efforts, initiatives, and actions—that will determine the quality and state of the country's neighbourhoods, towns, and cities in the future. This is why the exemplary role that Canada is capable of playing in the world of the future should begin at the municipal level in the geographical, cultural, and public sense. If it doesn't work at that level, it likely won't work at any other level.

CHAPTER NINE

Sustainable Culture—Dynamic Economy

T wo events occurred in 1904 that were destined to have a significant impact on Canada and Canadians. The first was the speech
given by Wilfrid Laurier that furnishes the theme of this book.
The second was the birth of Tommy Douglas.

Douglas surely heard of Laurier's speech in later years, as he spent the
bulk of his life in politics, and in any event he certainly got the message. This remarkable individual worked diligently for many years to
improve the health and well-being of Canadians. His political career
spanned four decades, including periods as an MP, MPP, leader of the
Saskatchewan Co-operative Commonwealth Confederation (CCF), and
leader of the New Democratic Party (NDP). He is often described as a
politician who was concerned first and foremost with people and their
problems and needs.

Medicare was undoubtedly Douglas's greatest achievement, since it
was the first government-operated health care plan in North America and
one of the first in the world. However, Douglas fought tirelessly for the
working class all his life, making valuable contributions to the development of the labour movement, unions, collective bargaining, and the realization of workers' rights in Canada.

Douglas was ideally suited to this task. He had grown up in a family
with strong ethical convictions, moral values, and religious beliefs. He also
experienced a great deal of poverty and hardship, first as a boy in Scotland
and later as an adult in Saskatchewan during the darkest days of the
Depression. Little wonder this pioneer of democratic socialism, fighter for
human rights and freedoms, and leader of Canada's first socialist government was once described as "a little giant of a man who stirred up Wey-
burn, the province, and the nation."

Canada is a more caring, sharing, and compassionate country as a
result of Douglas, with a great deal more commitment to the needs and

rights of others—especially the poor and the underprivileged—as well as more equitable distributions of income and wealth. Without Douglas's efforts and initiatives, Canada would not have the highly developed social welfare system it does today, since its creation was influenced by his remarkable vision, courage, and determination. Nor would it have a public health care system that is one of the finest in the world—a system that costs the country less as a proportion of GDP than would private health care, delivers better results, and remains a defining feature of Canada in the eyes of countless Canadians and people and countries in other parts of the world.

Like Tommy Douglas, Joseph-Armand Bombardier was also a very determined individual. He was born in Valcour, Quebec in 1907. About the same time that Douglas was working to improve social well-being in Canada, Bombardier was working to improve transportation and recreational capabilities in the country by inventing vehicles that could travel over the snow.

Both developments resulted from personal experiences and the environment the two men grew up in—for Douglas, the poverty and squalour he experienced in Scotland and later in Saskatchewan, and for Bombardier, the incredible snowfalls and snowdrifts that occurred in Quebec during the winter months. These snowfalls were so relentless that at times entire buildings seemed to disappear and many areas were cut off for weeks at a time.

Bombardier wanted to create vehicles that could overcome these challenges. He got his wish in 1922 when, at the age of fifteen, he took an old Ford car his father had given him, removed the motor, and attached it to the frame of a four-passenger sleigh. He then installed a huge wooden airplane propeller on the drive shaft and produced the first power-driven mechanical vehicle capable of travelling over the snow. This was the snowmobile.

Bombardier was granted a patent for his invention in 1937 and immediately started to produce snowmobiles commercially. This proved to be very successful. During World War II, he built similar vehicles for the armed forces. Then, in 1959, he created the Ski-doo, a snowmobile meant for personal and family use. It took Canada and the world by storm, adding a whole new dimension to the meaning of winter and "fun in the snow." He spent the rest of his life perfecting these and other vehicles, setting in motion a chain of events that has proven very beneficial to Canada, Canadians, and people and countries in other parts of the world.

Like Bombardier and Douglas, Tom Patterson was also a determined individual. He dreamt of creating a major arts festival in Canada—a Shakespearean Festival—after returning home from the Second World War. If a festival of this type could be created and flourish in William Shakespeare's home town of Stratford-on-Avon in England, why not a similar festival in Patterson's home town of Stratford, Ontario?

No one in Stratford thought this was possible. However, with the city's prosperity endangered by the downsizing (and eventual closure) of the rail yards that had sustained the town for so long, people were willing to give Patterson a chance. This was the opportunity he needed and immediately seized. After a long and seemingly endless battle, Patterson managed to convince Stratford City Council and other key civic authorities that his dream was not so far-fetched. Working closely with Dora Mavor Moore, the grand dame of Canadian theatre at the time, and with others professionals in the theatre community, Patterson eventually got in touch with Tyrone Guthrie, one of the world's greatest actors and directors.

Patterson, Moore, and others succeeded in persuading Guthrie to come to Stratford to assess the situation for himself. He liked what he saw, but there was a major problem. Stratford did not have a suitable facility to put on plays, so where would performances be held? After a great deal of discussion and debate, it was decided to open the first season in a tent. A huge canvas tent was ordered from Chicago and the first season opened on July 13, 1953. When Alex Guinness spoke those immortal words from Shakespeare's Richard III—"Now is the winter of our discontent / Made glorious summer by this son of York"—the Stratford Festival was born.

Things moved quickly after that remarkable first summer. A world-renowned theatre designer, Tanya Moiseiwitsch, was brought to Stratford to design the kind of amphitheatre and "thrust stage" that Guthrie envisaged. It was built in the parklands along the Avon River. Several world-famous actors and actresses such as Alec Guinness and Irene Worth were hired at the very outset to ensure that the Festival achieved a high level of excellence as well as a great deal of visibility and credibility. In the years to follow, many other well-known actors, including Alan Bates, Len Cariou, Martha Henry, Jessica Tandy, Brent Carver, Hume Cronyn, Lorne Greene, Maggie Smith, William Hutt, James Mason, Christopher Plummer, Peter Ustinov, Donald Sutherland, and Sarah Polley performed at the Festival. Many were Canadian, and quickly became household names in Canada and other parts of the world due to their success on stage and later on screen.

Stratford is not the only small town in Canada where some incredible feats have been accomplished. Florenceville, New Brunswick is another. Named after Florence Nightingale, the world-famous nurse, it recently amalgamated with Bristol to become Florenceville-Bristol. Situated in the northwest part of New Brunswick, it is located in one of the most beautiful spots in Canada—the Saint John River Valley—and has a population of some 2,000 people. What makes this town so special is the fact that it is the home of McCain Foods, the largest producer of frozen French fries in the world.

The roots of the company can be traced back to Europe. Several members of the McCain family left Ireland for Scotland and then emigrated to Canada in 1825 in search of a better life. They settled in New Brunswick. Eventually, four brothers, members of the third generation to live in Canada, founded the company; of them, Harrison and Wallace were most active in the business, and built it into one of the largest frozen food empires in the world, basing it on such core values as *authenticity* —"be real, open, and informal"; *commitment*—"create your future and be the vision"; and *trust*—"do the right thing."

There is a great deal to be learned from the lives, works, and achievements of these talented Canadians that is relevant to the creation of a comprehensive culture and dynamic economy in Canada in the remaining decades of the twenty-first century.

In the first place, Douglas, Bombardier, Patterson, and Wallace and Harrison McCain were all people who had visions of the things they wanted to accomplish, as well as the will, determination, and courage to make their dreams a reality. They also accumulated the personal and professional experience, as well as the foresight, enthusiasm, and commitment to a cause, that were required to create and deliver concrete results. For having a dream is not enough. Dreams must be made visible and tangible in some way, such as when Douglas created Medicare, Bombardier produced snowmobiles and the Ski-doo, Patterson founded the Stratford Festival, and the McCains founded their company.

Each of these individuals made a valuable contribution to Canadian culture by filling a fundamental gap. Douglas did so by addressing the health care and social welfare requirements of Canadians. While there was much discussion about the need for this prior to Douglas' arrival on the scene—including promises made by William Lyon Mackenzie King during the 1921 election campaign that he would create a new "social order" in Canada as well as the *Report on Social Security in Canada* that called for a comprehensive social security system—not much was achieved until Douglas began his work. Small wonder Douglas was chosen "the greatest Canadian of all" in a CBC poll.

What Douglas did for health care and social welfare, Bombardier did for winter transportation and recreation. Prior to the invention of the snowmobile and the Ski-doo, winter was a time that most Canadians endured rather than enjoyed. Not being able to get around easily during the winter months, they preferred to stay indoors rather than go outside. The invention of the snowmobile and Ski-doo changed this and opened the door to a very different attitude towards winter, especially in terms of the expansion of recreational activities such as snowmobiling, downhill and cross-country skiing, snowboarding, snowshoeing, tobogganing, tubing, and so forth. This had a powerful effect on the development of many winter recreational areas, trails, and ski resorts across the country, especially the Laurentian region and Mount Tremblant in Quebec, Banff and Lake Louise in Alberta, Whistler in British Columbia, and Blue Mountain in Ontario.

Then there is the Stratford Festival. It made a major contribution to another fundamental component of Canadian culture, namely the arts. While Canada had many professional arts organizations before the Stratford Festival was created in 1953, what the country did not have was a symbol of its coming of age artistically. The Stratford Festival provided this by proving that Canadians are as capable of producing arts organizations of international stature as anyone in the world. Nor was this all. The Stratford Festival proved that the arts and arts organizations are capable of transforming entire communities and providing important economic benefits.

This ability of the arts to act as dynamic catalysts for transformation and change is extremely important. While most political, corporate, and bureaucratic leaders believe the arts follow rather than lead economic development, the Stratford Festival proved that the reverse can be—and often is—the case, something that has been reinforced by the experiences of other towns and cities across the country such as Winnipeg, Vancouver, Edmonton, Niagara-on-the-Lake, Quebec City, Montreal, Halifax, St. John's, and Toronto. The Stratford Festival proved that the arts, rather than being a drain on the public purse, can reverse economic decline, stimulate employment and commercial possibilities, attract tourists and a skilled labour force, and revitalize communities.

Finally, there is McCain Foods, whose creation belongs to another crucial sector of Canadian culture, namely business and industry. It was fitting that this remarkable achievement took place in New Brunswick, since a similar development took place nearby in Nova Scotia many years earlier with Archibald Huntsman's development of frozen fish fillets for commercial use. McCain Foods was significant in proving that Canadians are capable of creating and developing major industries and are not just "hewers of wood and drawers of water" in the resource-extraction sector.

These four examples also prove something else of fundamental importance with regard to Canada, Canadians, and the exemplary role the country is capable of playing in the world of the future. In all four cases, significant contributions were made to the development of Canadian culture as well as the Canadian economy. And each initiative started out small and confined to a very specific geographical location, but grew in size, stature, and significance. For example, Douglas's work led over time to the creation of countless hospitals, medical and research centres, facilities and equipment, pharmaceutical companies, and so forth, all of which have generated billions of dollars in expenditure and investment. Bombardier's invention resulted in a whole new industry devoted to the production and sale of millions of snowmobiles and other recreational vehicles. In much the same way, Patterson's work triggered an incredible upsurge in tourist activity in and around Stratford and inspired similar arts initiatives in other communities. And the McCain brothers' venture resulted eventually in jobs for more than 17,000 people worldwide, global sales in the $10 billion range, the construction of more than forty-one sites on six continents, and the processing of millions of tons of potatoes.

Each of these individuals (and many others like them) was highly creative as well as extremely enterprising in the contributions they made. Not only did they break new ground in some fundamental way, but they also demonstrated a great deal of entrepreneurial expertise and a willingness to take risks and strike out in new directions. There is no doubt that these two qualities—*creativity* and *entrepreneurship*—will be of quintessential importance to the development of Canada, Canadian culture, and the Canadian economy in the years ahead. It follows from this that Canadians will have to invest far more heavily in the development of creativity and entrepreneurship in the future. There is a rich mine here waiting to be tapped, one that will pay handsome dividends for the country and its citizenry if done so fully and effectively.

What is equally apparent from these examples is the fact that Canadians no longer have to go abroad to develop their creative ideas and entrepreneurial talents. Nor will they have to rely as fully on foreign capital, markets, corporations, and other countries to translate their dreams into reality. It is possible to do so right here in Canada, with Canadians sharing in the profits. Clearly the country and its citizenry have come a long way since J.J. Brown was compelled to conclude after his intensive survey of Canadian inventions and inventors that "The story of Canadian invention and technology can be seen as a melancholy procession of golden opportunities which we have let slip through our fingers. We have let them go abroad to be developed by other nations because we have not had the vision to see their potential."

That Canadians possess the creativity, entrepreneurial talents, and vision required to develop these opportunities and take full advantage of them in Canada is a major step forward over previous centuries, when many of the country's most talented inventors, creative talents, and entrepreneurs were forced to live and work elsewhere and rely on American or European capital, markets, and companies to turn their ideas into realities. For what the lives and experiences of Douglas, Bombardier, Patterson, the McCain brothers, and a host of other Canadian creative and entrepreneurial talents confirm is that it is possible to live and work in Canada, develop creative ideas and entrepreneurial enterprises here, translate innovative ideas into concrete economic and commercial realities, and see Canadians benefit from the process. While it took time to bring to fruition the creative ideas and entrepreneurial initiatives of Douglas, Bombardier, Patterson, the McCain brothers, and many others, and while there were numerous disappointments and setbacks along the way, ultimately these obstacles were overcome.

Canada and Canadians are better off today as a result. So are people and countries elsewhere in the world. For the fact of the matter is that many creative ideas and entrepreneurial capabilities that have been cultivated in Canada have been embraced in other parts of the world. This is what people and countries in other parts of the world want from Canada and Canadians. They want products, processes, and technologies that are typical of this country, of its culture, and of Canadian creativity and entrepreneurship. Let's give them to them.

Canadians should be constantly scouring the domestic and international environment to identify those areas where Canadian creativity and entrepreneurship have a great deal to offer people both at home and abroad. Much of this creativity and entrepreneurship will be in areas where these qualities and capabilities have manifested themselves most profusely in the country in the past, such as transportation, communications, telecommunications, technology, resource development, science, engineering, the arts, public administration, health care, computer graphics, sports, recreation, and so forth. However, much should also be in areas that are under-represented or under-developed at present, such as energy conservation, advertising, marketing, branding, design, diplomacy, digital technology, and the development of international and multilateral relations. Suffice it to say here that there is a profuse array of internal and external opportunities in all these areas—and many others—that need to be explored and capitalized on in the future.

There is one final lesson to be learned from the examples of Douglas, Bombardier, Patterson, the McCain brothers, and others like them that must be addressed. It is that it is essential to develop *all* areas of Canadian culture, not just some areas. This is the key to developing a sustainable, comprehensive, and inclusive culture, as well as making the transition from wealth to well-being. If we can get right the development of Canadian culture in this holistic sense during the balance of the twenty-first century, everything will fall naturally and inevitably into place. While the Canadian economy is a core element in this process, it is only part of something substantially larger as well as more fundamental and profound: the development of Canadian culture *as a whole*.

The most conspicuous attributes of this culture are its creativity, diversity, and the fact it represents a distinct way of life. It is no longer a case of developing the Canadian economy and then assuming that everything will turn out for the best. Rather, it is a matter of developing Canadian culture in all its various forms and manifestations, and then ensuring that it is properly positioned in the natural, historical, and global environment as well as developed and administered effectively. Without this, it will not be possible to create a sustainable culture or dynamic economy in the future.

A few examples should suffice. If the country's environment and natural resources are not developed and managed effectively and harmonious relationships established between Canadians, nature, and "the land," a severe price will be paid in terms of environmental exhaustion and economic deterioration. If Canadians' educational needs are not met and the country's educational system is not successfully developed and integrated fully into the country's culture, both Canadian culture and the Canadian economy will suffer. If first-class social and health care programs are not developed and linked to other key aspects of the country's cultural life, Canadians' health will deteriorate. And if superb recreational, artistic, scientific, and spiritual amenities are not provided, Canadians will not be able to get the rest and relaxation they need to deal with the stresses and strains of modern life. Nor will they be able to savour the benefits that come from living in a free, democratic, and safe society, as well as a well-balanced and well-managed culture and economy.

Clearly when some parts of Canadian culture are well-developed and others not, or when some parts are over-developed and others under-developed, everything suffers. Too much economic growth consumes too many natural resources, produces too much pollution and waste as well as too many carbon emissions and greenhouse gases, and fails to conserve natural resources for future generations. Conversely, too little economic growth decreases standards of living, produces more unemployment and too few investment and market opportunities, and creates too much pressure, tension, and stress. Moreover, too few social programs make it impossible for Canadians to maintain a reasonable standard of health care and decent quality of life. However, too much government involvement in the country's culture and economy can dampen private initiatives and stifle Canadian ingenuity.

A culture must be created in Canada that is responsive to all the many different needs of Canadians. A fine balance must be struck and maintained between consumption and conservation, competition and cooperation, environmentalism and materialism, commercialism and spiritualism, and capitalism and socialism. Without this, Canadians will not be able to enjoy high standards of living, a better quality of life, and greater well-being. Nor will they be able to live creative, constructive, and fulfilling lives, or contribute to the realization of a better Canada and a better world.

This is what makes the development of Canadian culture in the holistic, equitable, and sustainable sense so essential. It is only when Canadian culture is "firing on all cylinders," so to speak, that the country's culture is fulfilling its most important mandate, namely to ensure that all Canadians have the resources, wherewithal, and opportunities they need in all areas of the country's cultural life to enjoy happy, healthy, and fulfilling lives and not just material wealth.

If this is the key to creating a sustainable culture in the remaining decades of the twentieth century, what is the key to developing a dynamic economy during this same time period?

Most importantly, it is essential to situate the Canadian economy properly in Canadian culture. This is necessary for three reasons. In the first place, it is required in order to see clearly how the country's economy fits into the overall picture, which can only be achieved by positioning the economy in a broader, deeper, and more fundamental cultural context. This will ensure that the country's economy does not take on a life of its own as has too often been the case in the past, thereby causing environmental problems and major disparities in income and wealth. This will also ensure that the necessary changes are made to the country's economy so that in the future it is dynamic and strong rather than static and weak.

In the second place, the Canadian economy must be imbued with human, social, aesthetic, humanistic, and qualitative values and not just material, monetary, technological, and quantitative values. This is especially important with respect to the distribution of income and wealth, since a small coterie of Canadians now owns and controls the bulk of Canada's income and wealth. Without substantial change, the needs of all Canadians and not just some Canadians will never be met.

Finally, we must take into account many factors, forces, and trends that are bound to have a powerful impact on the Canadian economy in the years ahead. Included here are the rapidly changing nature of employment, the technological revolution going on in Canada and around the world, the nature and direction of the world's major economies, including the Chinese, Indian, and especially the American economy, and the impact of global warming, an aging population, and other developments.

When these three factors are considered, it is clear that it is necessary to create an economy in the future that is *equitable, clean, green, creative, strong,* and *diversified.* It pays to examine each of these requirements in turn since they hold the key to transforming the Canadian economy in dynamic and progressive ways.

Creating an economy that is equitable is the most important requirement of all. This is needed not only for moral, ethical, social, and political reasons but also for economic reasons. As income inequalities widen, the lower and middle classes will not be able to make their full contribution to the Canadian economy because they will be too caught up simply trying to cope with the economic system rather than fully contributing to it. Recent initiatives undertaken by the federal government to stop the hollowing out of the middle class—most notably through the middle class tax cut and the Canada Child Benefit—represent an important step in reversing this undesirable trend. These initiatives should be reinforced and enhanced considerably in the future.

Creating an equitable economy is also important because of the enormous changes going on today with respect to the nature of work. Because of contemporary developments in communications, technology, automation, the replacement of labour by capital, the growth and power of multinational corporations, outsourcing, and artificial intelligence, work and employment will be very different in the future.

Several decades ago, most Canadians held only one or two jobs over the course of their lives. They were usually employed full-time, worked in factories or offices, and had a single lifelong occupation or profession. They also had a great deal of employment security, and were rewarded with reasonable pensions and other benefits if they performed effectively on the job and maintained their employment status.

Things are very different today for most Canadians. There is a great deal more temporary, part-time, contract, and precarious work. In addition, more and more citizens are working at home rather than in factories or offices, have several occupations rather than one, are compelled to move from one field to another, and enjoy less in the way of pensions and other benefits. As a result, a significant percentage of the Canadian population is experiencing a great deal of stress with respect to their employment situation and prospects for the future. It is difficult to know what jobs will exist in the future, how much income will be necessary to make ends meet, and what will be required to raise a family, own a home, and have a decent and enjoyable life.

This is why there is a great deal of discussion these days about the need for some form of guaranteed annual income. Since employment possibilities are less certain, some form of guaranteed income is needed to ameliorate Canadians' fears about making ends meet.

While there is much debate as to how a guaranteed annual income should be defined and what level it should be set at, there is no doubt that some form of guaranteed income is badly needed to ensure that the basic requirements of life for all Canadians and their families will be met and their survival guaranteed, regardless of their present employment situation. This would go a long way towards providing Canadians with the assurance they need that poverty and bare-bones survival will not be their future lot.

Some form of guaranteed annual income could also contribute a great deal to reducing income inequalities, improving health and health care, and strengthening social bonds and connections, especially if it were combined with policies aimed at raising the minimum wage to a more acceptable level, increasing social welfare and assistance rates, and enhancing the employment tax credit so that work is preferable to welfare. Also required is an overhaul of the country's employment insurance system and an effort to reduce poverty among those with insufficient means.[*]

While these measures would help to ensure a more equitable economy, much more is required. Given huge disparities in income and wealth, there is a need to achieve greater equality through a tax system that is more progressive and capable of redistributing income and wealth from the top five percent of Canadians, who possess or control most of the country's income and wealth, to the remaining ninety-five percent. The recent reduction in the middle income-tax bracket from 22 to 20.5 percent is a first step in the right direction, as would be closing various tax loopholes such as those revealed through the Panama Papers. The goal should be to overcome the persistent inequities that exist in income and wealth between rich, poor, and middle-class Canadians.

If greater equity is one requirement for building a dynamic economy in the future, so is creating a clean and green economy. The economic system of the future must be very different from that which exists today, and must be sustainable for future generations. This will require dealing effectively with climate change, as well as walking more lightly on the land and assuming responsibility for future environmental problems, developments, and directions.

The most immediate challenge here will be to "decarbonize" the Canadian economy. This means reducing carbon emissions well below their present levels. Globally, these efforts received a major boost with the signing of the Paris Agreement in 2015, as well the major agreement concluded in 2016 by some 200 countries to limit emissions of greenhouse gases that are even more powerful causes of global warming than carbon dioxide, such as fluorinated gases. The Pan-Canadian Agreement on carbon emissions reached by the federal government and the provinces and territories in December 2016 should also be mentioned, despite the fact that the Saskatchewan and Manitoba governments did not sign this agreement at that time.

Actions like these will have to be strengthened considerably by increasing the use of such energy sources as electrical, solar, fuel-cell, water, wind, and tidal power. (For instance, New Brunswick recently

[*] See, for instance, Carol Goar, "Sensible blueprint for a more equitable Canada" (*Toronto Star*, Wednesday, March 3, 2016, A13).

committed itself to harnessing the tides of the Bay of Fundy to generate electricity.) Fortunately, such developments are becoming more common, largely because major investors in Canada and other parts of the world are beginning to shift their holdings and investments into clean and green energies and technologies and out of fossil fuels.

Added to this are major declines in the price of solar panels, significant reductions in the cost of wind power, and the development of communities that are devoted to becoming "carbon neutral," such as Ashton Hayes in England and Eden Mills in Canada. As a result of such developments, Canada is now the fourth-largest producer of wind, water, and solar power in the world and the creator of numerous jobs in this area. But more is required. A national carbon price must be established and agreed upon by the federal, provincial, and territorial governments, and it needs to be substantially higher than the $30 per ton set by the government of British Columbia in 2016 to encourage the transition to a "decarbonized" economy.

Dealing effectively with the environmental crisis will also necessitate a greater focus on conservation. Canadians need an economy in the future that renews and revitalizes the natural environment at every opportunity and in every way, eliminates duplication and waste, rewards companies for exemplary environmental conduct, and leads the world in making the transition from consumption and production activities high in resource inputs and outputs to activities that are low in resource inputs and outputs. Such an economy should be based less on the production, distribution, and consumption of goods and services and creation of material and monetary wealth and more on human well-being in the social, aesthetic, spiritual, and qualitative sense.

There is also the need for the economy of the future to be much more creative. Many developments are required here for this to become a reality. Fortunately, there are some important precedents to capitalize on. As indicated earlier, Canada played a seminal role in promoting the idea of "the creative city" through the founding and development of the Creative City Network of Canada in Vancouver as well as the extensive research undertaken by Richard Florida at the Martin Prosperity Institute at the University of Toronto on what is called "the creative class." The time has come to make a similar contribution to the development of "the creative economy," which the United Nations Conference on Trade and Development (UNCTAD) recently defined as "an emerging concept dealing with the interface between creativity, culture, economics, and technology in a contemporary world dominated by images, sounds, texts, and symbols."

Situated squarely in the middle of this is the "creative sector" of society, which is seen by many as the spearhead and springboard that is needed to drive economic growth and development in the future. This sector consists of a coterie and clustering of creative people, talents, and activities in the arts, sciences, architecture, media, digital technology, marketing, design, the crafts, fashion, cuisine, and so forth. While creativity is not exclusive to these areas or this sector—as we have seen, it is manifested in other areas and sectors such as business, industry, agriculture, politics, government, sports, education, recreation, and so forth—it tends to be especially high in the creative sector because many extremely inventive people are attracted to this sector and work in it. Not only does this sector generate trillions of dollars in investments, expenditures, sales, and "market share," but also it triggers myriad opportunities and has important spin-offs effects on the more traditional sectors of the Canadian economy, especially resource development, manufacturing, and light and heavy industry.

Much contemporary evidence confirms that it is not possible to have creative towns, cities, regions, and economies without having a vigorous creative sector. This is because people working in this sector produce many of the concepts, contexts, ideas, brands, and so forth that are required to activate and stimulate other possibilities and prospects.

Just as Canada played an exemplary role in the development of transportation and communications systems in earlier periods of history, so it is capable in the future of playing an exemplary role in the development of the creative sector and the creative economy. In order to realize this goal, it will be necessary to invest heavily in Canadian invention, ingenuity, and innovation, undertake a great deal more research and experimentation, establish many more small businesses and commercial establishments, take many more risks, and ensure that the gains from expenditures and investments in these and other areas accrue to Canada and Canadians and not to people and countries in other parts of the world.

A good example of the problems that can be encountered in this area is illustrated by recent experiences in Canada's creative sector. Current research reveals that foreign media companies such as Netflix and YouTube are extracting millions of dollars from the Canadian economy in the form of subscription fees and advertising revenue. A similar situation exists in the newspaper and magazine industry, where comparable amounts are siphoned off every year by a variety of foreign digital media companies and platforms. This is resulting in the loss of revenues that could be used to create more Canadian jobs, films, television programs, books, recordings, magazines, newspapers, and other cultural activities and artefacts. This practice must be ended and replaced by policies, practices, and legislation that ensure that profits in areas of the Canadian economy like this accrue to Canadians and Canadian companies, industries, and creative talents.[*]

If developing a creative economy is necessary, so, too, is developing an economy that is strong and diversified. Historically, Canada has relied too heavily on resource extraction, thus running the risk of falling into "the staples trap" that Harold Innis and other economists have warned against. Unfortunately, this risk has reared its head once more over the last few decades, due largely to the signing of the North American Free Trade Agreement, the ubiquity of natural resources throughout the country, and the comparative advantage Canada enjoys over other countries in resource exploration, extraction, and exportation. Since the country has a significant proportion of its labour force tied up in resource development and the demand for Canada's natural resources will likely increase significantly in the decades ahead because of the expansion of the global economy and world population growth, what is required to prevent Canada and the Canadian economy from once again slipping into this staples trap?

Creating an economy that is much more fluid, forceful, and diverse is the key to this. This will only occur, however, when the Canadian economy is "firing on all cylinders," much like Canadian culture. In order to achieve this, it will be necessary to focus far more attention on developing "knowledge-based" and "value-added" industries—much as they are doing in Australia and other parts of the world—as well as providing a great deal more encouragement and financial support for "creative start-ups" as well as other entrepreneurial activities and initiatives.

Indeed, if there is one area where the Canadian economy comes up short, it is in high-end skills development, value-added industries, innovative start-ups, and the promotion and development of inventive industrial, commercial, manufacturing, and technological activities. If this situation is not corrected in the future, Canada will be at a competitive disadvantage compared to other countries.

If there is one place where all these needs and requirements converge and intersect, surely it is in the development of a highly progressive and

---

[*] For instance, see Kate Taylor, "We need to discuss why Canadian culture is a public good" (*The Globe and Mail*, Friday, February 5, 2016).

very sophisticated educational system. This is looming larger and larger as the key to developing a sustainable culture and dynamic economy in the future.

If this is to be achieved, Canada will need a first-class educational system at every level, from the earliest years of childhood to the final years of life. This means well-managed and well-cared-for schools, inspired and inspiring teachers, committed and enthusiastic students, excellent computer, digital, and electronic equipment and facilities, and numerous courses and programs in many different areas of cultural life. No Canadian should be deprived of an early, elementary, secondary, post-secondary, or adult education because of insufficient means, exorbitant tuition fees, prohibitive living expenses, expensive textbooks, computers, and learning materials, huge debts, or any other obstacle.

It is especially important for the country's young people to enjoy outstanding educational experiences and, once they finish their formal academic studies, stimulating employment possibilities. As things stand now, many Canadians in their late teens and early twenties are unable to find suitable and stimulating employment opportunities, either because jobs are not available, they lack the specific educational qualifications for the jobs that are available, or they are not well trained for the jobs that do exist. This situation must change dramatically in the future if the country's economy is to fire on all cylinders. Not only must sufficient educational and training opportunities be provided for young people, but more practical education and job-training must be provided by companies with full government support, as well as by other private and public sector organizations. Incredible benefits are being lost to Canadians and the Canadian economy every year because too many of the country's young people are not being prepared effectively for the future, are not able to make the transition from school to working life, or are floundering when their potential for learning is greatest and their energy highest.

As mentioned earlier, creativity and entrepreneurship are the keys to this. Not only must the country's young people be encouraged to be far more inventive in the educational system—largely through exposure to and involvement in such areas as the arts, technology, and the mass and social media where invention and innovation abound—but they also must be encouraged to be far more entrepreneurial in their studies and academic work. In order to do this, they should be exposed to the lives and works of Canada's most creative talents and successful entrepreneurs, some of whom were mentioned earlier in this book.

Adult education is another important area. Due to the rapid pace of life and escalating rates of technological and economic change, what is relevant and accessible today may not be tomorrow. Adults will need to continuously upgrade and update their skills and abilities. Many more adult educational opportunities will have to be created for immigrants and refugees so that they can be effectively integrated into, and make their full contribution to, the development of the Canadian economy and culture as a whole. Clearly, adult education, like early childhood education, should be to the twenty-first century what elementary, secondary and post-secondary education was to the twentieth century.

Thus far, we have been talking about what is needed to develop Canadian culture and the Canadian economy successfully in the remaining decades of the twenty-first century. But this is not only a "development problem." It is also a "management problem." If the country's culture and economy are not well managed, Canada will not prosper and Canadians will not make the breakthrough that is necessary to be exemplars in the future.

As indicated earlier, the management function is largely the responsibility of the country's governments. While citizens, community groups, corporations, foundations, educational institutions, and all the various sectors of Canadian society have an important role to play in the process of developing the country's culture and economy, it is the federal, provincial, territorial, and municipal governments that have the most important management role of all. They are the institutions that must have the all-inclusive and overarching perspective that is required to achieve this, as well as the power, authority, and mandate to carry it out, as provided in the Canadian Constitution and generally accepted by all Canadians. It follows from this that the country's governments must be the principal architects, overseers, and administrators of the country's culture and economy if they are to function effectively and meet the needs of Canadians for safety, security, survival, good health, and well-being in the twenty-first century.

Like every good architect, overseer, and administrator, the country's governments should monitor the development of Canada's culture and economy on a continuous and systematic basis, as well as ensure that they are meeting the goals, objectives, indicators, priorities, and outcomes that are created for them. This means transforming them in areas where they are deficient or ineffectual, as well as re-creating them in areas where they don't function properly. When the Fathers of Confederation made "good government" one of the three basic cornerstones of the BNA Act, they knew what they were doing. Without good government—governments that manage the affairs of the country and its citizenry with efficiency, effectiveness, and compassion—the country's culture and economy will not serve Canada and Canadians to best advantage in the future.

What is required for the country's governments to carry out this mandate? Surely the ability to act wisely, impartially, and in the public interest, as well as to exercise full authority and control over Canada's domestic and international affairs. Having examined what will be required for governments to carry out this task within the country, it is time to determine what will be required to do so upon the world stage.

CHAPTER TEN

Canada on the World Stage

T
here is a wonderful statue of Samuel Cunard that stands majestically overlooking Halifax harbour. From the glint in his eyes you can tell that he is gazing outward not just at the harbour but far beyond, to the Atlantic Ocean, England, Europe, and the entire world.

Beneath the statue in large, bold letters is an inscription that reads: *Samuel Cunard, 1787–1865, Haligonian – World Benefactor.* Further down, the inscription describes Cunard as a "visionary who foresaw steam power replacing sail power on the North Atlantic." It goes on to say that "the advent of steam on the North Atlantic forever altered commerce and communication between the Old and New Worlds." Indeed, the transition from sail to steam transformed water transportation throughout the world.

If Cunard is looking beyond Halifax harbour to the Atlantic Ocean and England first and foremost, that is no coincidence. His parents were United Empire Loyalists who came to Nova Scotia from the United States in 1783. Following in the footsteps of his father, who was also a marine pioneer, entrepreneur, and businessman, Samuel was obsessed with capturing the mail, trade, and passenger service between Nova Scotia and Britain, the British colonies in the West Indies, and the United States. While it took a great deal of time, effort, and marine experience and expertise, Samuel laid the foundations for building the Cunard Steamship Lines into one of the largest and most successful steamship companies in the world, famous for its reliability, outstanding service, punctuality, attention to detail, and comfort, as well as for launching some of the largest and fastest ocean liners in the world in the nineteenth and twentieth centuries.

England was quick to claim Cunard as its own, especially as Canada had yet to be created as a country. However, Cunard was in every sense a Canadian. He was born in Nova Scotia and spent the bulk of his life (and certainly all of his working life) there, creating a huge maritime empire that had a powerful effect on the whole world. His vision, determination, foresight, and commitment speak volumes about Canada and Canada's past, present, and future development. For much like Cunard, Canadians should be setting their sights on the entire world.

While Canada will always have strong ties with certain countries—most notably United States, England, and France—the entire world should provide the *context* and *container* within which Canada's international relations are developed in the future. Achieving this will lead to deeper relations with African, Asian, Latin American, Caribbean, and Middle Eastern countries, as well as a more balanced and comprehensive approach to international relations and foreign policy.

The key to all of this lies in capitalizing on the fact that Canada is a microcosm of the global macrocosm. This is apparent both at home and abroad. At home, Canada's population is extremely diverse in its composition and character. This makes it possible for the average Canadian to come into contact with people from virtually every part of the world on a daily basis, as well as to experience numerous multicultural events and activities in the country's towns, cities, provinces, territories, and regions. Abroad, Canada is rapidly gaining a reputation throughout the world as a truly multicultural country—the *first* real multicultural country in the world in the official, political sense. Canada is now well-known as a place where people from every conceivable part of the world can preserve their customs, identities, traditions, and cultures—as well as their beliefs, values, and ways of life—while still being an integral part of Canadian culture as a whole.

In view of its ethnic, demographic, and linguistic diversity, Canada is in an ideal position to play a powerful role in the world of the future. As a middle power with few aggressive tendencies, the country and its citizenry are not interested in imposing their will, values, culture, or political convictions on other people or other countries. This gives Canadians a great deal of credibility in the world, especially if they can solve their domestic problems and maintain a strong commitment to peace, order, good government, caring, sharing, respect for cultural differences, and the needs and rights of others.

Canada possesses strong ties and connections with most if not all parts of the world as a result of its historical development and bilateral and multilateral relations. Consider Africa. This vast continent of incredible variety and complexity has aroused the interest of many Canadians in the past, from the days of the Boer War to more recent contributions by Prime Ministers Lester Pearson, John Diefenbaker, and Brian Mulroney in helping to address racial violence, conflict, and apartheid in Africa in general and South Africa in particular. Canadians have also provided assistance during the famines that continue to plague some African nations. One should also mention the role that General Roméo Dallaire played in endeavouring to come to grips with genocide in Rwanda by becoming a passionate spokesperson for resolving ethnic conflicts and ending human rights abuses (much as Project Ploughshares did in the horn of Africa for many years), as well as the part played by Stephen Lewis in bringing the HIV/AIDS crisis in Africa to the world's attention when he served as a special advisor to UN Secretary-General Kofi Annan.

As a result of these and other developments, Canada has a great deal of credibility in Africa. This credibility should be used to advantage in the future, especially as many African nations need help in areas where Canada possesses expertise and experience, such as resource and energy development, the creation of transportation, communications, and tele-communications systems, governance, public administration, and the provision of health care, educational, and social services.

Because of past experiences and present developments, Canada has even stronger ties and connections with Asia and Asian countries—especially in southeastern Asia and with "mega-nations" like China and India—than it does with Africa. The economic achievements of India over the past few decades are remarkable, and have been called a miracle by many a "world-watcher." The concept of "village-by-village development" has worked well in India on the whole, as has the revolution going on today in communications, information technology, film, entertainment, and social media. This comes at a time when the number of Asian citizens in Canada is growing rapidly, not only people from India but also from China, Pakistan, Bangladesh, Vietnam, Singapore, and many other countries.

The business acumen and political expertise of people from this part of the world who are now living in Canada are being increasingly recognized and rewarded as they move from the wings to the mainstream of Canadian economic, political, scientific, and academic life. Although the Commonwealth, which was for many decades a major player on the international scene, has virtually vanished from sight in recent years, members such as India and Pakistan still have fond memories of the close association with Canada and Canadians that proved beneficial on numerous occasions. Canada played an active and important role in the development of this remarkable institution, and by virtue of this and other developments, now enjoys many opportunities to engage in a great deal more trade, exchange, and bilateral and multilateral relations with these countries.

Then there is China. With its huge population, it continues to move inexorably and inevitably towards becoming a genuine superpower. With fewer ideological constraints, increased technological skills, a gigantic home market, and myriad other developments, there is no doubt that China will play a far more powerful role in the world of the future than it did in the past.

Fortunately, the name of Norman Bethune still resonates strongly with many people in China, largely for the valuable contributions he made to China during the many years of famine and destitution as well as during the difficult wars with Japan. Although there is little willingness in China today to accord any special status to the contributions of missionaries from Western countries, as ideology fades and more objective historical interpretations and accounts emerge, the "good works" of many Canadian doctors and missionaries such as Dr. Robert McClure, who spent a quarter-century in China (from 1923 to 1948) as a medical missionary and outstanding surgeon, will be an important asset in building new partnerships, alliances, exchange agreements, and opportunities with this rapidly emerging superpower. Moreover, the diplomatic courage that Canada demonstrated in according early political and diplomatic recognition to the People's Republic of China also helps to place Canada and Canadians in a much stronger position to engage in relations with this country in the future.

Developments like this are being strengthened and enriched by the rapidly expanding number of Chinese immigrants who have come to Canada from Hong Kong, Taiwan, and the Chinese mainland over the last fifty years. This is providing a great window of opportunity for more trade, interaction, and a constellation of economic, social, commercial, and educational benefits for Canada and China alike. Chinese Canadians, like other ethnic groups in Canada, are also forming many new associations in Canada, ones that will stand them and Canada in good stead on a variety of fronts in the future. A leadership is rapidly emerging in Canada that possesses the necessary Mandarin, Cantonese, and other linguistic skills to provide the basis for many more federal, regional, and municipal trade and diplomatic possibilities with China in the future. It is not surprising in this regard that trade and commerce between Canada and China have increased significantly in recent years.

Although other Asian countries such as Korea, Singapore, and Japan have not received the same degree of attention accorded China by Canadians, they should also figure prominently in the minds and plans of Canadians in the future. Canada's West Coast will become the front door to these countries in the twenty-first century as the centre of gravity in world relations shifts from west to east.

While Canada has had relatively few historical and contemporary connections with South America, Central America, the Caribbean, and Mexico—apart from tourism, and, of course, Mexico's participation in NAFTA—there exists enormous potential to increase Canada's dealings with these countries. With an increasing number of immigrants coming to Canada from Argentina, Chile, Ecuador, Peru, Venezuela, Brazil, Columbia, Mexico, Jamaica, Trinidad, Costa Rica, and elsewhere in this area— not to mention refugees from these parts of the world who have come to Canada to escape political turmoil and persecution—Canada is in an ideal position to capitalize on new opportunities, especially in countries like Brazil, which is rapidly emerging as a major player in South America and appears destined to play an important role in the world of the future because of its geographical size, large population, and abundant resources. The fact that many immigrants to Canada from this region speak Spanish and Portuguese should help considerably in strengthening Canada's economic, technological, educational, social, and artistic ties with these parts of the world in the years ahead.

This brings us to the Middle East. While Canada's large Jewish population will ensure close and sustained ties with Israel, the fact that an increasing number of immigrants and refugees are coming to Canada from other Middle Eastern countries suggests that Canada will become much more involved in this region in the future. Canada's role must extend well beyond developmental assistance, refugee resettlement, and occasional intervention in strategic issues to embrace humanitarian causes that may also lead to closer economic relationships, as well as increased cultural understanding of and dialogue with this part of the world. It is one thing for Canada to shift assistance in the Middle East from air and ground attacks on ISIS or Daesh targets and strongholds to more effective training of local personnel; it is quite another to assist these countries in attempting to come to grips with dictatorial rulers, oppressive regimes, centuries-old grievances, and fundamental differences in religions and politics.

Finally, there is Europe and the United States. Because historically most immigrants to Canada have come from these parts of the world,

Canada has strong ties and close connections with most European countries and especially with the United States. There is every reason to believe that much stronger ties and connections can and should be developed between Canada and these parts of the world in the future in every area of the country's cultural life, from agriculture, industry, and military affairs to social developments, the arts, sciences, education, sports, the environment, and so forth. These relationships will have to extend well beyond what has been achieved in the past, with a view to substantially increasing the volume and value of trade and investment, negotiating more artistic, scientific, and educational exchanges, participating in a variety of safety and security measures, pursuing environmental preservation and planning, and so on. This is especially important with respect to the United States, with which Canada has strong ties in both the historical and contemporary sense, regardless of what political party is in power in the U.S.

Canada's long experience with multiculturalism in general and ethnic and cultural diversity in particular will prove very helpful in developing productive and profitable international relations in the future. The country and its citizenry have gained immensely from the large and well-established ethnic communities that now exist throughout Canada. Most of these communities have maintained close links with family members, friends, relatives, and organizations back home.

The fact that Canada has appointed a number of Governors General representative of various ethnic communities will also be helpful. Especially symbolic in this respect were the appointments of Edward Schreyer, representative of the German community, Ray Hnatyshyn, representative of the Ukrainian community, Roméo Leblanc, representative of the Acadian community, and, perhaps most importantly, Michaëlle Jean, representative of the Haitian community, and Adrienne Clarkson, representative of the Chinese community.

And this raises a very interesting question. What other country in the world would appoint people to one of the highest and most prestigious offices in the land who were born in another country, as were Jean and Clarkson, and who were refugees as well? Acts like this, and many others related to Canada's commitment to multiculturalism and pluralism, have not gone unnoticed in other parts of the world.

If Canada is to capitalize on these multifarious benefits and opportunities, the country's international sector will have to be expanded well beyond its present size. As indicated earlier, this sector is severely underdeveloped compared to the country's domestic sector and to the international sectors of most other Western countries, primarily because historically most of Canadians' energy and attention went into creating a sovereign and independent country against virtually insurmountable odds, as well as developing a robust economy and providing a high standard of living and excellent quality of life for the country's citizens. Since these goals were achieved largely by focusing on the country's domestic development and capitalizing on its profuse supply of natural resources, not a great deal of attention was given to Canada's external relations.

This was compounded by the fact that Canada was for many centuries dependent on France and England (and more recently the United States) in terms of its political, diplomatic, and military affairs and relations with other countries. This is why an expansion in this area is so vital. Not only will it make it possible to achieve balance between the country's internal and external development, but it will open the doors to a "quantum leap" in Canada's international relations and foreign policy, enhancing the enormous opportunities that exist in this area.

If achieving this and "getting square to the world" are imperative if Canada is to play a major role in the world in the future, so is seeing this role from a holistic and cultural perspective, rather than a partial economic, commercial, or political perspective.

Looked at from a holistic and cultural perspective, Canada engages in international relations in order to achieve a variety of objectives. Some of these objectives have to do with advancing the interests of Canada and Canadians, while others have to do with advancing the interests of people and countries in other parts of the world and of the world as a whole. The problem is that these objectives seldom coincide, and are so interwoven, interconnected, and interrelated that it is difficult to differentiate among them.

Generally speaking, however, Canada's international relations can be subdivided into two major components when considered in cultural or holistic terms. On the one hand, there are relations that are designed to advance the interests of Canada, Canadians, people and countries in other parts of the world, and the world as a whole in *material and concrete* terms. Included here are such objectives as improving the Canadian economy and living standards of Canadians; overcoming domestic resource deficiencies; expanding the realm of consumer and producer choice; taking advantage of agricultural, industrial, technological, financial, and trade possibilities; generating tourist opportunities; advancing the interest of business; and so forth. These are usually described as "hard" objectives because they are intended to produce tangible benefits and outcomes. Most of these benefits can be measured in exact terms and are quantitative in nature.

In contrast to this are international relations designed to advance the interests of Canada, Canadians, people and countries in other parts of the world, and the world as a whole in other ways. Most of these ways involve objectives that are far more *humanitarian, humane,* and *benevolent* in character. This includes improving the quality of life of Canadians and people and countries in other parts of the world; easing tensions between the different peoples, cultures, religions, countries, and civilizations of the world; realizing more peace, security, stability, order, and harmony in the world; curbing conflict, violence, war, terrorism, and oppression in specific parts of the world; creating more happiness, fulfillment, and contentment in people's lives; improving the state of the natural environment; helping the less fortunate; promoting academic, artistic, scientific, social, and humanistic causes and endeavours; and enhancing diplomatic relations between countries, continents, and civilizations. These are usually referred to as "soft" objectives and are much more difficult to pin down because they are more intangible and qualitative in nature. However, this does not mean that they are any less important.

Complicating this situation is the fact that there are countless interactions between these two basic components of Canada's international relations. For example, humanitarian initiatives may help ease tensions between Canada and other countries so that Canada can enjoy greater trade opportunities. On the other side of the ledger, practical and concrete relations may open up humanitarian and benevolent possibilities.

The situation is further complicated by the fact that international relations affect Canada and other countries in different ways. Increasing trade with countries in Africa, Asia, South America, the Caribbean, and the Middle East, for instance, may not do a great deal to advance Canada's and Canadians' economic interests. However, it may do a great deal to advance the economic interests of the aforementioned countries and the world as a whole. In much the same way, helping to diffuse political, religious, and military tensions and hostilities in the world—such as those in and between Middle Eastern countries—may do little to advance Canada's international interests and objectives. However, it may prove extremely helpful, if not absolutely crucial, in enhancing the lives of people in other countries.

To this must be added the fact that actual harm can be done when some of Canada's economic interests are pursued in other countries or parts of the world with little sensitivity for local conditions—for example, when certain types of logging, mining, and industrial operations are conducted in other countries. A good example involves South America, where Canadian logging and mining interests have been pursued in certain cases with little concern for the needs and interests of people in this part of the world. International relations are seldom straightforward. Inconsistencies, conflicts, and complications can and often do arise that must be taken into account.

Matters are made even more complex because Canadians in general— and Canada's political parties and politicians in particular—often have conflicting views about what is in Canada's best interests and what objectives should take precedence. Despite these challenges, and many others that might be cited, Canada has evolved a system of international relations and foreign policy over the last century and especially over the last fifty years that is on the whole balanced and effective, even if it is limited in scope and has not produced as many benefits for Canada and Canadians as some would like.

Many of the country's hard objectives have been met, such as stimulating the Canadian economy and increasing the volume of trade. Moreover, many soft objectives have also been achieved, largely through foreign aid and developmental assistance provided to African, Asian, Latin American, and Caribbean countries, despite the fact that these efforts have fallen short of what some other Western countries have done as well as currently accepted standards. These efforts have been complemented by a number of peacekeeping missions and other initiatives, thereby contributing to the well-being of other people and countries through the work of such organizations as the Canadian International Development Agency, the Canadian Council for International Cooperation, the International Development Research Centre, and many others.

There are many reasons why this system with its delicate balance between hard and soft objectives should be enlarged, enriched, and cultivated much more aggressively in the future. In the first place, doing so is consistent with the country's historical experience. As a result of being able to walk the fine line between the two diverse sets of objectives and satisfy the interests of Canada and other countries, Canadians have been able to develop an excellent reputation in most if not all parts of the world. Canada and Canadians are not seen as a country and a people obsessed with their own interests and needs, but as a compassionate and caring people and country who are also concerned with the needs and interests of other countries, people, and the world as a whole. This has contributed significantly to Canada's credibility in the world—credibility that places the country and its citizenry in an ideal position to play a much more powerful and exemplary role in the world of the future.

But Canada's excellent reputation will be tarnished if this system is not enhanced and cultivated more fully in the future. This was made crystal-clear between 2006 and 2015. By placing a much higher priority on hard as opposed to soft objectives in international relations—largely by linking international relations to the realization of economic and financial benefits while downplaying environmental and humanitarian concerns—the Conservative government pushed matters to the point where Canada lost respect in the world. Many Canadians were relieved when Justin Trudeau announced at the United Nations that "Canada is back" shortly after his government took office in 2015, sending a clear signal that Canada was returning to its more traditional role in world affairs.

While these reasons for enhancing Canada's system of international relations in the future are sufficient in and of themselves, there are even more compelling reasons why doing so is imperative. *These reasons have to do with the exemplary role Canada and Canadians can and should play in the world of the future.* It is the type of exemplary role that the Liberal government played in establishing gender equality in the federal cabinet. While this was only one act of exemplary conduct, it proved that countries do not have to have a great deal of political power, economic clout, or military might to play this type of role. All they have to do is stand up for principles and ideals that resonate strongly with people and countries in other parts of the world—and put those principles and ideals into practice. The fact that many politicians and countries throughout the world recognized this act on the part of the Canadian government and expressed a desire to follow suit confirms that leadership can be exercised by less powerful nations.

Without doubt, such exemplary conduct is desperately needed in the world of the future. The world needs a country and a citizenry that will stand up and be counted on crucial issues; that will put the needs and interests of other countries, other people, and the world as a whole ahead of their own when necessary and appropriate; that will strike a judicious balance between the hard and soft objectives of international relations; that will show compassion and respect for the less fortunate; that will confront multinational corporations, wealthy elites, and powerful establishments when their practices are misguided or self-indulgent; that will act as a model for other countries by creating modes of behaviour, life-styles, and ways of life that conserve rather than consume resources and protect rather than damage the natural environment; and that will seek justice, harmony, equality, and peace for all people and countries.

In order to manifest behaviour and achieve ideals like these, Canada and Canadians will have to act as global leaders. This is especially important with respect to climate change and the environmental crisis, despite the many nay-sayers on this matter. Boasting a long line of environmental activists, advocates, pioneers, and conservationists, as well as being responsible for one of the most successful international environmental accords in history (the 1987 Montreal Protocol), Canada has an obligation to play a leading role with regard to environmental reform, regulation, and protection.

The country and its citizenry can achieve this obligation and responsibility by creating targets that lead the world in greenhouse gas reductions, playing a central role in future conferences and summits dealing with environmental reform, and working out effective agreements between various levels of government on environmental issues that will serve as models for other countries and their local, regional, and national governments. This should be augmented by actions that lead the world in making the effective transition from outdated industrial technologies and fossil fuels to renewable energy sources, expanding investments in clean and green energy, and most importantly, reducing the huge ecological footprint Canada and Canadians impose on the planet's natural environment.

If acting as a global exemplar on environmental issues is imperative, so is increasing foreign aid and developmental assistance to the point where Canada sets the standard for the world.

Canada has a long way to go to achieve this in view of present commitments. In the final decades of the twentieth century, foreign aid and developmental assistance as a percentage of Canada's gross domestic product stood at roughly one-half of one percent. While this made the country a world leader at that time, expenditure on foreign aid and developmental assistance later dropped to a low of just under one-quarter of one percent of GDP, and now stands at approximately 0.28 percent. This is far below the goal of one percent of GDP for "developed" countries advocated by Lester Pearson and the Pearson Committee in its well-known *Partners in Development* report of 1970. It is also well below the goal of 0.7 percent espoused by the United Nations and most international agencies and authorities—a goal achieved only by Great Britain and a few Scandinavian countries as world leaders in this field today.

Canada's goal in this area in the future should be the one percent of GDP advocated by the Pearson Committee. While it will take time to reach this figure, which is more than three times the present level, this level of assistance is desperately needed in today's world. While foreign aid has not been a major political priority in Canada over the last few decades, it should be a major political priority in the future. It is time for Canada and Canadians to step up and be counted on this issue, much as they did in the past when this level of commitment was required, including fighting in two world wars and responding to a number of major humanitarian crises, such as taking in thousands of Vietnamese and Syrian refugees.

The principal focus of Canada's foreign aid and developmental assistance in the future should be on improving the welfare and well-being of the poorest countries and peoples of the world. This does not mean that Canada should be cavalier about the way it distributes and delivers foreign aid. Considerable care should be exercised to ensure that aid and assistance are allocated equitably and judiciously and produce concrete, long-term results. Desirable outcomes should be clearly identified and defined; standards of performance should be rigorously enforced; programs and procedures should be carefully monitored and fully evaluated; and tough assessment measures should be established and applied. Through this process, Canada should become an international exemplar in developing new forms of foreign aid and developmental assistance as well as fresh criteria of effectiveness, and not simply a global leader in terms of its contribution as a percentage of GDP.

While foreign aid and developmental assistance have an important role to play in improving living standards and the quality of life for the poorest peoples and countries of the world, an equally important role must be played by Canada's international development organizations. Due to the historical and contemporary character of Canadian development, Canada possesses a wealth of expertise in areas that are of vital importance to the welfare and well-being of people and countries in Africa, Asia, Latin America, the Middle East, and the Caribbean. Through organizations such as CARE Canada, Doctors Without Borders, Oxfam Canada, World Vision, Canadian Crossroads International/Carrefour Canadien International, CUSO, SUCO, CESO, the Primate's World Relief and Development Fund, the World University Service of Canada, Save the Children Canada, the Aga Khan Foundation, Inter-Pares, and others, this expertise should be made available to countries and people in less fortunate parts of the world on a much larger and more sustained basis.

These efforts should be augmented by programs that reduce—and hopefully eliminate—oppressive debt loads for African, Asian, Latin American, and Caribbean countries. While some of these debts result from legitimate expenses incurred by countries as they endeavoured to over-come difficult developmental problems, the levels of debt are often so oppressive that they make it impossible for these countries to break out of the "development trap" and end the cycle of poverty and despair. Every time some light appears at the end of the tunnel it is snuffed out by exor-bitant interest payments that are far beyond the capacity of these coun-tries to pay.

To this must be added debts that result from loans that go directly into the hands of powerful elites and dictators, as well as loans made to finance inappropriate megaprojects tied to corrupt corporate and political regimes. Canada could play an exemplary role here by spearheading an international movement aimed at coming to grips with the practices that produce these debts in the first place.

Having considered foreign aid and developmental assistance, it is possible to turn our attention to trade, one of the most important elements in Canada's future system of international relations. Canada is, and likely will always be, heavily dependent on trade with other countries. Not only does international trade constitute an indispensable element in the devel-opment of the Canadian economy, but it is essential in improving the well-being of Canadians and people and countries in other parts of the world.

Viewed from the holistic perspective provided by culture, what is of greatest concern about Canada's present trade situation is the country's heavy dependence on the United States. This dependence has reached alarming proportions in recent years, largely as a result of the close proximity of the two countries and Canada's participation in the North American Free Trade Agreement. While this situation has produced many benefits for Canada, there have also been many drawbacks. According to the Council of Canadians, Canada has lost more than half a million man-ufacturing jobs since NAFTA was signed in 1993.

Canada's overdependence on trade with the U.S. leaves the country vulnerable to fluctuations in America's economic and financial fortunes as well as to various types of political and diplomatic pressures that can infringe upon Canada's independence. If Canada does not go along with major American economic, military, or political initiatives or interests, there is the inherent risk of some form of retaliation through restrictions on Canada's trade opportunities with the U.S. It is all very subtle but it is always there lurking in the background, just as it does for all countries that live beside powerful neighbours and are dependent on them economically.

This is not a viable scenario for Canada in the future. If Canada is to play a exemplary role in the world, it must reduce its economic dependence on the United States and be careful not to become too dependent on any other single country. The solution to this problem lies in greater international economic diversification. In order to achieve this, the federal government should work closely with provincial, territorial, and municipal governments, as well as the private sector, to formulate and implement the short-, medium-, and long-term policies, practices, strategies, and tactics that are necessary to diversify Canada's trade relations. This will provide the balance that is required to maintain Canadian sovereignty and independence.

Is it possible to achieve this and still remain in NAFTA? Surely it is. But in order to do this, major changes will have to be made to NAFTA. This is especially important when it comes to control over natural resources, as well as improving Canada's manufacturing prospects and possibilities. If Canada and the Canadian economy are to be fully developed and managed effectively in the future, the country will have to possess full control over its natural resources as well as the capacity to increase its industrial output substantially. Without such control, Canada will find that its future trading capabilities will be impeded at the very time that the world experiences shortages in natural resources.

This helps to explain why Canada has been pursuing other trade possibilities and agreements, most notably the Canadian-European Union Comprehensive Economic and Trade Agreement (CETA). This trade agreement was signed by Canada in principle in 2016 and encompasses some 500 million people. Massive trade agreements like this have their benefits, but they also have their problems. As Linda McQuaig pointed out, although some improvements were made to this agreement, the process was "deeply flawed" since "special privileges for investors, known as Investor-State-Dispute-Settlement (ISDS), remain essentially intact. Investors will still be able to bring lawsuits over government policies they don't like, and their lawsuits will still be decided by special tribunals where they will enjoy stronger legal protections than are available to any other group in domestic or international law."

What McQuaig went on to say strikes at the heart of this matter and should be of great concern to all Canadians, both now and in the future:

[D]espite the revisions, CETA will undermine Canadian democracy, handing foreign corporations a powerful lever for pressuring our governments to, for instance, abandon environmental, health or financial regulations, while leaving Canadian taxpayers potentially on the hook to pay billions of dollars in compensation to some of the wealthiest interests on Earth.*

It follows from these and other developments that if trade agreements don't work for Canada—and if corporations and investors are not accountable to governments, people, and the public trust—those agreements should not be signed at all or should be renegotiated if they have been signed. There should be no room in Canada's future international relations and trade policies for commitments that work well for other countries but not for Canada.

And this brings us, via a rather circuitous route, to the profound transformation that is going on in many parts of the world today from free trade to protectionism. After many decades of relentlessly pursuing free trade and signing various types of free trade agreements, some countries are now indicating that they are anxious to pull out of such agreements or renegotiate them, as well as to build protective walls around themselves and establish tariffs and policies that protect domestic industries and prevent those industries from relocating in some other part of the world.

This trend in most conspicuous in the United States, where the Trump administration rejected the Trans Pacific Partnership, indicated an interest in pulling out of NAFTA or totally revising it, and says it wants to retain existing industries at home, penalize companies that leave the U.S., and attract foreign companies to the United States. And what is happening in the United States is happening in other countries as well, including Britain's decision to leave the European Union. While the reasons for these developments are complex and have strong nationalistic and populist overtones and implications, there is no doubt that they are changing the character of the global economic landscape quite considerably.

This shifting of the sands with respect to free trade and protectionism has a long history and can be traced back to the days of mercantilism in

---

* *Toronto Star*, Thursday, Sept. 1, 2016, p. A17.

Great Britain if not even earlier. In a nutshell, it always comes down to this. As long as free trade works for countries, they favour it. However, as soon as this is not the case, protectionism is the desired alternative. In the case of United States, the rise of protectionist sentiment is due largely to the fact the U.S. has been steadily losing ground to its rapidly evolving competitors, particularly China but also India, Mexico, and other countries.

This shift from free trade to protectionism has major implications for Canada since it dramatically alters the context within with Canada's international relations and foreign policy take place. Should Canada follow the example of the United States, as it has often done in the past, and reject free trade in favour of protectionism? Or should it pursue its present policy of free trade despite the American rejection of it? While Canada has lost its fair share of jobs and manufacturing market share because of free trade, it should continue to pursue free trade as long as the costs don't get out of hand. This course of action is what is needed to play an exemplary role in the world, as well as to achieve and maintain the delicate balance that is required between the hard and soft objectives of Canada's international relations and foreign policy. It is difficult to see how this can be achieved if the country gets mired in protectionist policies and practices that involve breaking away from other countries rather than opening up to them, especially as protectionism usually invites retaliation and eventually everyone loses.

Just as embracing free trade and signing NAFTA put Canada on a very specific path, so did the events of September 11, 2001, and the many other developments since that time that are connected to Canada's safety, security, and defence.

While the war on terrorism caused the United States to rely much more heavily on unilateral strategies and actions as well as on a large military build-up to protect itself against rogue states and internationally based terrorist organizations and activities, Canada has remained resolute in its determination to deter threats to its security through well-established processes and channels that are based largely on multilateral commitments, including commitments to the United Nations, NORAD, and NATO. This means, and should always mean, renouncing militarism and the "fortress mentality" that the "go it alone" attitude tends to encourage, as well as rejecting any belief that attacks from abroad should be prevented through destructive and expensive weaponry and a commitment to revenge, retaliation, and retribution.

Canada's defence and security system is based primarily on the conviction that major hostilities in the world—despite the best efforts of the United Nations and other international organizations and agencies to come to grips with them—are fundamentally connected to poverty, weak economies, high rates of unemployment, homelessness, and the lack of hope that encourages the creation, recruitment, and arming of terrorists and terrorist organizations with extremist beliefs and a determination to wreak havoc on the affluent nations of the world. Clearly Canada should not make a contribution, commitment, or concession to defence policies or security procedures based on *excessive* military force as the way to peace, safety, security, and defence.

However, if Canada's voice is to be heard and respected in such matters in the future, Canada must assume its fair share of responsibilities in this area and pay the real costs associated with them. While the emphasis on peacekeeping and peacemaking requires a different complement of armed forces, skilled and well-trained military personnel on the ground, and the capacity to provide all of this at a moment's notice in situations where civilian populations are in danger, this is incredibly expensive. So, too, is the need to protect Canadian borders, shorelines, and waterways from the Atlantic to the Pacific and the Arctic from invasions from abroad, as well as from possible terrorist and criminal elements. A significant amount of the cost of all this in the past and at present has and is being borne by the United States. This practice must be brought to an end and in the future Canada must pay a larger percentage of the cost of ensuring its own defence, although this transition will not of course occur overnight.

The same holds true for control of the country's air space, the defence of which is largely the responsibility of NORAD, for which the U.S. covers by far the greatest share of the cost. Canada should bear a reasonable portion of this cost as well. Borders, shorelines, waterways, skies, and airways have special meaning not only in terms of safety, security, and defence, but also in terms of international separation and political sovereignty. Canada should not expect the United States to provide protection to Canadian citizens in such matters. There should be no "free ride" on the American defence budget—or the development of a single North American defence system if discussions move in this direction—without an acceptance by Canada of the necessary responsibilities of nationhood, citizenship, and sovereignty.

In the process of working out its strategies and commitments in international relations, Canada should engage in activities that draw fully on its most powerful assets and capabilities and bring them to the fore in global development and world affairs. One such capability is obviously peace-keeping and peacemaking. The fact that Canada has a great deal of credi-bility in the world means that other countries trust Canadians to be honest brokers in resolving disputes and forging commitments to peace. This is an area where Canada's experience can and should be used to great advantage in the years ahead. Given such achievements as the Canadian Charter of Rights and Freedoms and the country's involvement in the creation, signing, and promotion of UNESCO's Convention on the Protec-tion and Promotion of the Diversity of Cultural Expressions, there is an opportunity for Canada to help other countries with the formulation and implementation of policies and initiatives regarding minority groups, human and gender rights, multicultural management, the protection of ethnic, cultural, religious, and linguistic diversities as well as local, regional, and national identities, the enactment of social legislation, assistance with elections, governance, civil administration, and educational reforms and developments.

What is true for bilateral relations is equally true for multilateral rela-tions and foreign policy as a whole. Over the last few decades, Canada has been involved in many matters aimed at advancing multilateral relations and international affairs, such as the elimination of land mines, reform of the United Nations administrative system, establishment of the Inter-national Criminal Court, world disarmament based on common security measures for all countries, and many other matters.

The emphasis on culture and the crucial role it can and should play in the conduct of Canada's international relations has special significance here and should not be ignored. Culture's emphasis on holism, values, the maintenance of customs, traditions, and heritages, and the realization of unity, harmony, and cooperation is especially important. So is culture's ability to decrease levels of violence, conflict, and confrontation.

This is what places Canada and Canadians in a strong position to make constructive and substantial contributions to the world of the future. The country's history and contemporary experience and its commitment to peace, order, good government, caring, sharing, cooperation, and diversity make it possible for Canadians to play an exemplary role in the world by opening up the visions and vistas and creating the bridges and networks necessary to address human needs in peaceful and harmonious rather than provocative and confrontational ways. To discount the importance of culture in international affairs and the seminal role the country and its culture can play in the world of the future would be a disastrous mistake.

In a world that is becoming increasingly volatile and violent, Canada occupies a position of unique importance. The country may have been a colony of France and England earlier in its history and overly dependent on the United States today, but there is no doubt that it provides many concrete and specific examples of how law, order, cooperation, compromise, peace, and harmony can be achieved in the world of the future.

And what is true for culture in general is equally true for Canadian culture in particular. As John Ralston Saul said many years ago:

> Canada's profile abroad is, for the most part, its culture. That is our image. That is what Canada becomes in people's imaginations around the world. When the time comes for non-Canadians to buy, to negotiate, to travel, Canada's chance or the attitude towards Canada will already have been determined to a surprising extent by the projection of our culture abroad.*

Nothing projects Canadian culture abroad better than the work of Canada's artists and arts organizations. Everything is there in one form or another: the many different languages spoken throughout the country; the cornucopia of cultures that have been created over the centuries by all the diverse peoples and ethnic groups that constitute the Canadian population; and especially the values and ideals that Canadians hold most dear. This is why a report on a major conference held in Halifax called "New Conversations" concluded that Canada's arts and cultural industries play a central role in "projecting the country's image as an open, dynamic, and creative nation." It ended by saying, "A cultural image sells itself, its country, and its products."

The same sentiments were echoed by Peter Donolo in a *Toronto Star* article entitled "Branding Canada would be money well spent." Donolo argues that what makes Canada so important in today's fractured and edgy world is "[o]ur stability. Our inclusiveness. Our civility and fairness. Our essential post-national sensibility. People around the world look at us and they see the future—or rather, the best future. It's our moment. Let's

*John Ralston Saul. *Culture and Foreign Policy: Canada's Foreign Policy: Principles and Priorities for the Future: The Position Papers.* Special Joint Committee of the Senate and of the House of Commons Reviewing Canadian Foreign Policy. Ottawa, November 1994, p. 85.

seize it."* And with these thoughts we are brought back to Samuel Cunard and his statue in Halifax. It is no coincidence that directly beneath the statue of Cunard is the inscription "world benefactor." For in the process of doing what he was intended to do, Cunard made an incredible contribution not only to what would become Canada, but also to the entire world. It was a contribution that served not just his own needs and the needs of his family and the colony in which he lived, but also the needs of the world at large and humanity as a whole.

This is the challenge facing Canada and Canadians. In the process of becoming an independent, forward-looking nation, Canadians have created the potential and wherewithal necessary to create not just a better Canada, but also a better world. This is why Canada has a unique role to play on the world stage in the remaining decades of the twenty-first century.

---

* "Branding Canada would be money well spent," *Toronto Star*, Friday, September 9, 2016, p. A13.

CHAPTER ELEVEN

It's Time to Lead

I t is not difficult to get caught up in the idea that the twenty-first century could belong to Canada. What Canadian would not be excited by this possibility?

However, most Canadians would regard such a prospect as little more than wishful thinking, given how many countries there are in the world and what is required for an entire century to "belong" to a single country.

Nevertheless, Wilfrid Laurier was not indulging in wishful thinking when he made his famous speech to the Canadian Club in 1904. Nor was Robert Borden, leader of the Opposition, when he responded to Laurier's speech by saying, "It may be through the mists I can even now discern the future greatness which I am sure will place this Canada of ours not only in the forefront of the nations of the Empire, but in the forefront of the nations of the world."

When Laurier made his speech, he saw many developments taking place that might make his prediction a reality. What he did not see, however, were all the profound changes going on in the world that would make the twentieth century the "American century," in the words of Henry Luce. Of course, predicting the future is always a "guessing game": no one knows for sure how events will unfold.

Nonetheless, there are some interesting signs that suggest the twenty-first century could belong to Canada under certain circumstances, and that Canada could play a leadership role in the world of the future, not as a seat of empire or a superpower, as were Britain in the nineteenth century and United States in the twentieth, but as an exemplar of things to come.

That is what this book is about. We have discussed the capabilities Canadians have built up over the centuries that could in the future prove timely and valuable both for Canada and for other countries. We have also considered problems looming up in the world that all people and all countries will be compelled to confront in the decades ahead, problems that are converging rather than diverging at this particular stage in human history.

In creating a strong and independent country against incredible odds, Canadians have manifested a great deal of creativity, dealt effectively with diversity, made concessions and compromises as necessary, and evolved a distinct way of life. The capabilities developed through these achievements could prove helpful to people and countries elsewhere in the world as they struggle to create higher standards of living and a better quality of life, build societies rooted in diversity, tolerance, inclusion, and cooperation rather than uniformity, intolerance, exclusion, and conflict, exhibit more caring, sharing, and compassion, and develop ways of life that are indigenous and authentic rather than imposed or imitative.

Canadians will have to build on all the capabilities they have developed over the country's history in order to survive and thrive in the world of the future. But for the country to play an exemplary role in the world, for the twenty-first century to truly belong to Canada, much more will be needed. It will be necessary to make some fundamental changes in the country's values, lifestyles, and overall way of life, as well as to strike out in bold, new, and very different directions in the future.

Particularly important is the need to transform the relationship between human beings and the natural environment, deal with climate change, reduce the huge disparities that exist in income and wealth, counteract terrorism, address social injustice, come to grips with demographic changes, provide more opportunities for young people, women, and marginalized groups, improve relations between the world's diverse peoples, ethnic groups, countries, cultures, religions, and civilizations, and enhance the prospects for peace, stability, and security in the world.

How well Canada addresses these challenges at home and abroad will determine whether the country is capable of playing an exemplary role in the world.

The key to doing so lies in developing Canadian culture as a whole, making the transition from wealth to well-being, and placing a high priority on the development of the public sector and public-sector institutions, services, and programs in the years ahead.

Developing Canadian culture as a whole is the most essential requirement of all. For in the final analysis this is what Canadian development is really all about, even though up until now the country's culture has been treated largely as an afterthought and in an unconscious rather than deliberate and systematic manner. Surely Gandhi was right when he said that "a nation's culture resides in the hearts and in the soul of its people." Conceived of in this way, culture encompasses all activities that Canadians engage in as they live their lives and address their needs. While the Canadian economy is an integral and indispensable element of Canadian culture as a whole—this fact will never change—it is part and parcel of something substantially broader and deeper as well as more fundamental and profound. Clearly all activities that Canadians are involved in—from agriculture, industry, science, technology, and politics to education, the arts, humanities, sports, recreation, and social affairs—will have to be developed successfully in the future if Canadians want to live happy, healthy, and fulfilling lives and enjoy high standards of living and an excellent quality of life.

Developing Canadian culture in this all-encompassing, holistic sense is essential for other reasons as well. It focuses attention on the big picture and not just particular aspects of it, and therefore on what is needed to situate the country's culture properly in the natural, historical, and global environment and achieve balanced and harmonious relationships between its many different parts. This is necessary to deal with all aspects of the environmental crisis, not just climate change, and to conserve and strengthen the country's cultural heritage and make it accessible to all Canadians. It is also necessary in order to expand the country's external sector and enhance relations with other countries, and to ensure that the Canadian economy meets people's needs and has a human face. Sustainable development—development that takes into account the needs of the natural environment and future generations and not just those of the present generation—can only be achieved by changing the context within which Canadian development takes place.

Making the transition from wealth to well-being is an indispensable part of this process as well. If Canadians are to reduce the demands they are making on the natural environment, such a transition is imperative. It can only be achieved by putting more emphasis on activities that conserve rather than consume resources and that are labour-intensive rather than material-intensive in nature, since this is what is required to create a more effective balance between the quantitative and qualitative dimensions of Canadian development. In order to realize this, it will be necessary to fund and develop the arts and humanities much more broadly and fully, as well as put a great deal more emphasis on the social and spiritual aspects of life.

Placing a high priority on the development of the public sector and public-sector institutions, services, and programs is the final requirement in this transformative process. It is needed to realize a better balance between the public sector and the private sector, as well as to come to grips with numerous public-sector responsibilities and ensure that people and the public trust take precedence over corporations, profits, the marketplace, and the bottom line.

The Fathers of Confederation knew what they were doing when they made peace, order, and good government the ideals of the Canadian constitution. Unlike the American ideals of life, liberty, and the pursuit of happiness that are largely individualistic and private-sector ideals, the ideals embodied in the Canadian Constitution are primarily public-sector values, concerned with such matters as stability, security, harmony, citizenship, government, governance, and especially the public trust. While changing directions and priorities in the decades ahead should be a basic concern and fundamental responsibility of all Canadians, the country's governments and especially the federal government have a strategic role to play in this area by setting this transformative process in motion and ensuring that it is steered in the right direction.

This will not be possible without reducing Canadians' huge ecological footprint, coming to grips with inequality, focusing on the responsibilities of Canadians and not just their rights, improving early, adult, and cooperative education, addressing the injustices done to the Indigenous peoples and other minority groups, improving the employment prospects for young people, and dealing with many other needs that are the principal concern of Canada's federal, provincial, territorial, and municipal governments.

Many developments confirm that the country's governments are moving in a positive direction in this regard. Foremost among these developments are active participation in the Paris climate change agreement, creation of a pan-Canadian climate change framework, arrangements for a national carbon tax, commitments to developing cleaner and greener sources of energy, and changes to the tax system meant to address inequality.

If Canada's governments are to be successful in charting a new course for the country and making it operational, comparable and compatible developments will have to occur in the private sector. These include generating much more innovation and entrepreneurship, capitalizing on the creativity of all Canadians, increasing expenditures on research and development, particularly in digital technologies, rebuilding the manufacturing sector, and a great deal else.

If these and other developments occur, Canada will send out a strong signal to other countries that it intends to move in a more sustainable direction and play a far more dynamic and powerful role in the world of the future.

But even more will be required if the country is to play an exemplary role in the world. Canadians will have to steer a different course than that taken by the United States while still remaining good friends with our American neighbours. They will have to assert full control over the country's natural resources despite strong pressures from other countries and major corporations, stand up and be counted on a variety of humanitarian issues and social concerns, stick to principles, policies, and practices that may be unpopular and resisted in other parts of the world, renegotiate trade deals on a more equitable basis, substantially increase foreign aid and developmental assistance, and pay for a greater share of Canada's defence and military requirements rather than relying on the U.S.

Even more compelling will be the need to sustain Canada's commitment to multiculturalism and diversity at a time when many countries seem to be moving in a different direction, tightening up immigration procedures, and pursuing policies predicated more on uniformity than diversity. Doing so may prove to be the biggest challenge of all facing Canada and Canadians as they seek to play an exemplary role in the world.

If the United States' mantra going forward is "Make America great again," Canada's should be "Lead rather than follow." This is what will be required in the years and decades ahead to capitalize on our strengths and differences, appreciate and celebrate our similarities, come to grips with our shortcomings, and bring the country together rather than split it apart.

If the country and its citizenry can stand up and be counted on matters of conscience and character, it is quite possible that the twenty-first century *will* belong to Canada and that Canadians will play an exemplary role in the world during the remaining decades of the century. To do so would be to make a remarkable contribution to the world at a crucial time in human history.